Praise

Desperate Prayers

"Captivating. Encouraging. Challenging. If you read only one book on prayer this year, make it *Desperate Prayers*. Rachel Wojo skillfully writes with biblical wisdom, tender transparency, and gut-level honesty about the transformative power of prayer. At the end of each chapter you'll find prayer principles that should be framed and memorized. This is a not-to-be-missed book that will forever change the way you pray."
　　—**Carol Kent**, founder and executive director of Speak Up
　　　　Ministries, speaker, and author of *He Holds My Hand:*
　　　　　　Experiencing God's Presence and Protection

"In this transformative book, Rachel Wojo grabs your hand and leads you on a prayer-filled journey to exchange panic for peace."
　　　　　　—**Mark Batterson**, *New York Times* bestselling
　　　　　　　　author of *The Circle Maker*

"What do you do when your heart is so broken and burdened that you can't even find the words to pray? Rachel Wojo has been there and come out on the other side. With the tenderness of a compassionate friend and the tenaciousness of a fighting warrior, Rachel shares personal stories of hope and gives practical and powerful action steps to move you from desperate to expectant. I love this book!"
　　—**Sharon Jaynes**, bestselling author of twenty-six books,
　　including *When You Don't Like Your Story: What If Your*
　　Worst Chapters Could Become Your Greatest Victories and
　　Praying for Your Child from Head to Toe: A 30-Day Guide
　　　　to Powerful and Effective Scripture-Based Prayer

"We all experience desperate moments where we feel lost, abandoned, or forgotten. We have moments of great loss and terrifying fear. And we have small moments of simply wondering if God sees us or hears us. Because of this, we need this book. Rachel Wojo has been there, and she shares much-needed wisdom on these pages."

—**Jill Savage,** host of the *No More Perfect Podcast* and author of *Real Moms . . . Real Jesus*

"*Desperate Prayers* is a heartfelt and inspiring testament to resilience and faith. Rachel Wojo, with her vulnerability and strength, reminds us on every page that God is always present and always providing, even in life's toughest moments. This book is a must-read for anyone seeking encouragement and proof that prayer can transform every aspect of your life."

—**Katie Fisher,** executive director and founding pastor of Rock City Church in Columbus, Ohio

"From page one, Rachel gave me permission to feel my pain. But then she pointed me to hope. This is not another book of Christian platitudes on how to make it through difficulty or despair; these are the tender words of a friend who is holding out her hand to help hold you up. When you don't know what to say or where to turn, you don't know what to do, and you feel helpless or hopeless, this book is the answer you've been waiting for. Help is here."

—**Erica Wiggenhorn,** international speaker and author of *An Unexpected Revival: Experiencing God's Goodness through Disappointment and Doubt* (Moody Publishers)

"Are you in a desperate place struggling to find the words to pray? If so, *Desperate Prayers* is the resource you need. With empathy and vulnerability, Rachel Wojo shares her own despairing pleas and God's loving responses. She has discovered firsthand the power of prayer and encourages us to believe in its transformational power too. Through biblical and real-life examples, Rachel serves as a guide in your darkest moments. This book will renew your faith and invigorate your prayer life—changing your heart and circumstances."

—**Rachael Adams**, sought-after speaker, host of *The Love Offering* podcast, and author of *A Little Goes a Long Way*

"In *Desperate Prayers*, Rachel Wojo delivers a powerful and inspiring guide to help you trust God's heart and believe in His power. Rachel teaches you how to communicate with God for everything you need: comfort, guidance, freedom, miracles, and so much more. Her heartfelt words and practical advice will lead you to a deeper reliance on God, no matter what challenges you face."

—**Jennifer Dukes Lee**, author of *Growing Slow* and *It's All Under Control*

"Rachel has written a collection of stories that are balm and salve to the soul. We all grieve, and when we do, Rachel's words are a warm blanket offering advice and application, comfort and calm. This book is a reminder of the biggest power we possess: prayer."

—**Bryan Crum**, author of *Neighbor, Love Yourself*

"Raw, honest, hopeful—these three words came to mind as I devoured this book in two sittings. Rachel draws heavily from the heart-breaking death of her daughter and her own wrestling with God during Taylor's degenerative disease. Yet, in the midst of deep grief and confusion, Rachel turns pain into purpose and weeping into wisdom as she shares powerful lessons with us. As soon as I finished this book, I immediately turned back to the beginning so I could review all of my highlights I'd made."

—**Scott Savage**, pastor, author, speaker, and YouVersion partner

"I know what it is like to be in a desperate place with life in the balance and to have Rachel Wojo pray for you! In *Desperate Prayers: Embracing the Power of Prayer in Life's Darkest Moments*, you will be encouraged like a dear friend is lifting you and your need up to our Abba Father, and you will get equipped to be the kind of faithful friend who prays for others when life becomes a challenge."

—**Pam Farrel**, author of sixty-one books, including the co-author of *Men Are Like Waffles, Women Are Like Spaghetti* and *Discovering Hope in the Psalms: A Creative Bible Study Experience*

desperate prayers

desperate prayers

Embracing the Power of Prayer in Life's Darkest Moments

RACHEL WOJO

Skyhorse Publishing

Skyhorse Publishing books may be purchased in bulk at special discounts for sales promotion, corporate gifts, fund-raising, or educational purposes. Special editions can also be created to specifications. For details, contact the Special Sales Department, Skyhorse Publishing, 307 West 36th Street, 11th Floor, New York, NY 10018 or info@skyhorsepublishing.com.

Visit our website at www.skyhorsepublishing.com.

Please follow our publisher Tony Lyons on Instagram @tonylyonsisuncertain.

10 9 8 7 6 5 4 3 2 1

Library of Congress Cataloging-in-Publication Data is available on file.

Cover design by Chris Pochiba
Cover photo by Steph Jordan Photography

Print ISBN: 978-1-5107-8162-7
eBook ISBN: 978-1-5107-8163-4

Printed in the United States of America

Dad,
You taught me to work hard,
modeled a life of loving all types of people,
sent me to college, though you'd never had the privilege,
sacrificed to prioritize your family's needs,
and fostered a deep love for God's Word through your example.
To say I am grateful is not enough.
All my love,
until we meet again.

CONTENTS

Introduction

Not everyone has $5,000 in answered prayers dropped in their backyard. I can hardly believe I did.

Have you ever wondered if God answers prayers today? Does He still work miracles in people's lives like He did in the Bible? You know, the classic stories: the Red Sea rescue, Daniel in the lions' den, Jonah in the belly of a whale. Moses, Daniel, and Jonah experienced *big* answers to *big* prayers. But ordinary, everyday people who live in the twenty-first century? Could we possibly see answers to our prayers?

And why doesn't God answer "yes" to every request? I've heard the statement, "There are no big sins and little sins. All sin is sin." Does that mean there are no big prayers and little prayers? Does God see all requests at the same level? What constitutes an urgent prayer on God's timetable? I don't know about you, but my sense of urgency rarely matches God's. I'm like a toddler on the verge of a potty accident: "Daddy, now!" Especially in out-of-my-control circumstances.

When we can't see that a solution is on its way, our minds spin with confusion. Desperation ushers in pain, and grief soon follows. We plead with God, "Where's *my* miracle?"

The more I have studied the Bible, the more I have realized the men and women who cried out to God in deep despair echoed the cries of my own heart. Amid the words and groans of anguish, I discovered that frenzied desperation could be transformed into dependent faith.

If you picked up this book because you're pleading with God for an answer to your prayers, then you're in the right place. Would you recognize your miracle if it came packaged a little differently than you anticipated?

Over the decades, God and I have wrestled through many desperate seasons together. The "big D" spaces of discouragement, depression, divorce, disease, and death are personally painful and familiar places I've discussed with Him. I've experienced miraculous answers—and questioned why other prayers seemingly went unanswered. Through it all, I've learned that difficult circumstances can prompt divine conversations with a life-altering perspective.

My prayer for you as you read this book is that you'll begin to recognize and embrace God's peace, presence, and power in your prayer life as desperation fuels your dependence on Him.

CHAPTER ONE

The Cry of Distress

God, See Me.

A ping rang out as I swiped the dish towel across the final
dinner plate, and an unknown number popped onto the
screen. I glanced at the text.

*Rachel, you don't know me, but a friend has left a gift
for you. Please go to your backyard and look for a yellow
envelope underneath the green balance beam.*

My mind raced with possibilities, most of which were negative. Dare I open the back door? Maybe I should grab the pepper spray first. Yet, a sense of peace settled over my heart. This wasn't your typical "click here and win a million dollars" hoax. Whoever had sent the text knew my number and my name.

I slipped on my shoes and cautiously walked across the patio toward the balance beam my husband, Matt, had made for our two youngest girls. The stars and landscape lighting created enough light in the gathering darkness to guide my steps. I grabbed the envelope and sprinted into the house, straight to the garage where Matt was working.

"Honey, read this." I shoved the phone toward him. His eyes flitted over the text, then met mine. Hands shaking, I ripped open the envelope to find a typed letter.

Matt, Rachel, and family,
The angel of the Lord found (you) in the wilderness, Genesis 16:7.
Our Lord SEES you. Nothing escapes His notice.
Know that this is His provision. It is a demonstration of
His faithfulness, a reward for your faithfulness.

That was it. Typed. No name. No signature. In addition to the letter, the yellow envelope held a bank envelope. My heart pounded at its thickness. I tore open the seal, and our heads spun at the stack of cash that spilled out. I'd never held that much money in my entire life.

"Someone surely left us a lot of money!" As I fanned the bills, Matt and I realized only the first five were twenty-dollar bills. The rest were one-hundred-dollar bills—forty-nine of them.

Someone had left $5,000 in our backyard.

And I knew that someone was God.

The Wild, Not-So-Wonderful Wilderness

Have you ever felt like you've been deserted in the wilderness? I don't mean the one with cacti and sand, but a season of life that left you in serious need physically, mentally, emotionally, or spiritually.

Yep. I thought so. All humans on the planet experience desert places in our lives, but some seasons are incredibly rugged.

In March 2020, when the COVID-19 pandemic hit hard in the United States, thousands of people lost their jobs. Going without income, even for two weeks, would result in a significant financial setback for most people—but some folks went for months without paychecks. In my daily prayer time, I thanked the Lord that Matt, our children, and I were employed and earning income because I knew many weren't experiencing that kind of stability.

In 2021, when many of those unemployed people returned to the workforce, Matt came home from work as usual. But after just a bite or two of dinner, he said, "I have something I need to tell you."

From the moment he had walked in the door, I could sense he was discouraged. His eyebrows alone revealed this wasn't going to be good news.

The words tumbled out of his mouth. "I was let go today."

Shock and disbelief hit me like a tsunami. *Why? How? My husband is hard-working in everything he does.* This happens to others with poor work habits or unstable environments, or so I thought. But it had never happened to us, not even through the first months of a worldwide pandemic and statewide economic shutdown

After a flash of thoughts, unexplainable peace washed over my heart. Then, finally, I managed to say, "I don't understand it, but somehow, I know this is part of God's plan."

For more than two years before that moment, I had prayed for a new job for Matt. The daily corporate environment and challenges of his industry stressed him beyond what he should be enduring. Often, I begged the Lord to move him.

Maybe you're thinking, *Rachel, do you really think your husband getting fired was an answer to prayer?*

Yes, I do. I'm typically low-key until you mess with one of the people I love. Then mama-bear mode unleashes. I didn't know I possessed an internal mama bear until I had my first baby. I quickly discovered God equips parents with a sixth sense that spreads from parenting to protecting anyone we love. I felt certain that God had allowed this job termination because of the peace I felt in my heart about it. I believe God answered my prayer through this strange, challenging circumstance because Matt and I had been praying for a miracle when it happened.

Dictionary.com defines a miracle as "an extraordinary event manifesting divine intervention in human affairs." Miracles are out-of-the-ordinary circumstances. My husband had never been terminated from any position he'd ever held before. My choice to believe God worked in our lives through that circumstance was made in faith. God and I had enjoyed a proven prayer relationship for more than two decades at that point. He orchestrated details in my life, then gave me a front-row seat to watch miracles unfold. While this job loss was not my preferred answer, I felt confident He had answered prayer through this strange situation.

That day launched a wilderness season for our family that lasted eight months before Matt landed temporary employment. Who can go unemployed for that long without profound impacts? We had five kids at home to feed and clothe. There are little things called mortgages, car payments, and utilities that don't care what else is going on. So, although my initial response to Matt's announcement was peace-filled, my faith wanted legs to stand on—you know, something tangible I could touch with my hands and see with my eyes.

God and I chatted about that job loss, but initially, it wasn't an amicable conversation. I did most of the talking and, well, sobbing. (I'm so glad God is OK with ugly crying.) Thankfully, He carried the weight of listening.

In my heart of hearts, I wanted to know that He saw our family in that unexpected and empty place.

The Need to Be Seen

I've watched my husband teach our children to ride a bike. That special moment when they realize they can pedal independently and keep their balance is priceless.

My youngest daughter didn't want anyone to help when it was her turn. Rather than accept her daddy's support while she practiced, she procrastinated. She must have grown tired of our encouragement to learn, because two months after she turned six, she went out to the garage and jumped on the bike. Once she started pedaling, she didn't stop. Shocked, I managed to catch the show on video. She looked like she had known how to ride a bike her entire life.

Her bright eyes met mine with a huge smile, and she yelled, "Mom, look at me!"

It wasn't enough for her to enjoy the moment on her own. She needed to be seen.

Humans need to feel affirmed in their pain or pleasure. Helen Keller once said, "I would rather walk with a friend in the dark than alone in the light."[1] Imagine how well she understood this, having been both blind and deaf since she was nineteen months old.

The need to be understood and accepted lies at the forefront of our emotional well-being. As humans, we crave validation. When circumstances spiral outside our control, we throw baseline prayers of "God, do You see me? Do you know what is happening down here?" We strive to have Him recognize our situation and emotions, whether we are angry, hurt, or frustrated. Our natural bent toward resolving a conflict is the same intuition that rises in times of fear. We want to get out of distress, and basic instinct kicks in. We can choose to stand and fight or run in flight.

Genesis 16 explains Hagar, an enslaved Egyptian woman, faced this same choice and ran. Her mistress, Sarah, who was infertile, had forced her to sleep with her husband, Abraham, and Hagar became pregnant. Hagar resented her owners, and the situation spiraled downward like a reality TV show. Sarah mistreated Hagar, so she ran away—to the wilderness, of all places.

Can you blame her? Imagine Hagar's emotions, including loneliness, shame, and rejection. And possibly rage as well.

An angel of the Lord found Hagar by a spring in the desert, and the first thing he said was her name. "Hagar, where have you come from? Where are you going?"

Why is it unusual that the angel called her by name? In Genesis 16:1–3, we read that each time Sarah or Abraham refers to Hagar, she is called "my slave" or "your slave." Not once is she called by her name. Her owners considered her property, not a person.

What a beautiful moment for Hagar to be called out personally by the angel, an elevation from a possession to an individual. How special to be recognized as more than the label she carried!

Interestingly, she only answered one of the angel's questions: "Where have you come from?"

"I'm running away from my mistress, Sarah," she said. She most likely didn't answer the second question, "Where are you going?" because she didn't know. She had no plan. She was simply running.

Do you see yourself in Hagar? Maybe you think of yourself as the roles you fill, and you long to be seen as more than "John's wife" or "Susie's child." You carry many labels and wear multiple hats, but deep within, you long to be known. You want to be recognized for who you are.

Who are you, then? You are a child of the Most High King. God created you as a unique individual for a specific purpose. There is only one of you in the whole wide world, and only you can do the job for which God created you. God knows every hair on your head, and your name is engraved in the palm of His hand.[2] Every time you call to Him in prayer, He calls your name as the angel did to Hagar. "(Your name), there you are. I'm so glad you've called." Your cry does not go unnoticed. Just as the Lord saw Hagar's situation, He sees the challenges you and I face today.

The angel followed his questions by giving Hagar news I doubt she wanted to hear: "Go back."

I would have a few choice words with an angel if he told me to return to a situation where I was being mistreated. However, there's no record of Hagar's objection. Whether or not her heart was at peace with them, she followed the angel's instructions.

Drama over, right? No. Genesis 21 tells us Hagar lands in the wilderness again. Can you relate? When familiar distressing circumstances have arisen, have you ever prayed, "God, why am I in this situation again?" I wonder if Hagar thought the same.

This time, Abraham had sent her packing because Sarah did not want her son to share an inheritance with Hagar's son. Not only was Hagar in despair over still being mistreated, now she was also responsible for her son. When the water she had taken with her into the wilderness ran out, so did Hagar's strength. She left her boy under a bush and turned away because she could not watch him die. So he was crying, and I bet she was crying too. Have you ever passed a mama in the grocery store whose child is wailing to the stars? She looks like she wants to break down in tears too, right?

Hagar's prior wilderness experience repeated itself when the angel showed up again.

We don't know if Hagar's "cry of distress" began as a few words thrown upward in prayer, or if all she could do was cry without spoken words. We're not privy to the exact details of her prayer, nor whether she even uttered one. But we know she cried in pain, her son cried, and God heard them both. I imagine Hagar must have been reminded of her earlier wilderness experience, when the angel told her to name her son Ishmael, meaning "God hears."

It's easy to use desperate cries to God as last-measure prayers. You've heard it said, "All we can do is pray." When those words come out of my mouth, I immediately feel conviction. I want to replace that phrase with, "The *best* thing we can do is pray." While I know there are sit-

> *Prayer is the first pick, not the final straw.*

uations when there is nothing we can do in our human strength and prayer is our only option, I don't want to think of talking to God as a last defense. Prayer is the first pick, not the final straw. Rather than feeling all I can do is pray, I want to remember that prayer is one of the strongest tools in my spiritual arsenal.

But in Hagar's example, we see no condemnation for her outpouring to God. There was no "buck up and dry the tears" speech from the angel. No, the angel was there to give her a personal message of affirmation. Whenever she would call her son to meals or tuck him into bed at night and whisper his name, she would be reminded: *God hears me. His ear is ever tuned to listen for my cry and move to action on my behalf.*

Hagar memorialized her first angelic encounter with a name of her own choosing: From that moment on, she referred to God as El-Roi, "the God who sees me." This woman had experienced being heard and seen by her Creator and no longer questioned His existence. Her cry for help resulted in a deeper relationship with Him; not only did she realize that God saw her, but she also knew that she had seen God (Genesis 16:13). Hagar is the only person in the Bible to use this intimate name for God. How special is that!

I wonder how long it would have taken for Hagar to feel heard and seen if she hadn't met God in the wilderness.

9-1-1 Prayers

When my husband came home without a job, I knew the temptation I faced. Like Hagar, I wanted to run—not from my husband, family, home, or God, but from God's call on my life to write for Him. Writing is hard work, and contrary to popular belief, it's not exactly lucrative. For the last two decades, every time our family has faced a financial issue or setback, the enemy whispered, "Just get a real job. Clock in, clock out, get paid, and enjoy the benefits.

You won't have to worry about creating a steady entrepreneurial income or the next book contract. It will be easier." But I knew that God had heard me whenever I cried out to Him in the past. He knew about the job loss before I did. Like Hagar in the wilderness, I longed to see Him working through our family's dilemma. Desperation filled my heart, and I asked the Lord to transform the distress into fuel to pursue Him more deeply. I needed to hear His voice, providing direction and guidance for daily living. I'll confess that my prayers resembled 9-1-1 prayers.

When you dial those three numbers, you aren't thinking about how that call will make you feel; you just want help and help *now*! But the 9-1-1 operator who receives your call has a job to do when you dial in. First, she must establish a connection with you and immediately say something like, "I am here with you." Her job is not to solve the emergency in one sentence; her priority is to establish a connection as she dispatches the proper responder so she can help until the first step of the solution reaches you.

Confirming that we are not alone is central to handling the emergency in a crisis. Dr. Henry Cloud says, "When we are afraid, the first thing that calms the brain down and reduces stress is a feeling of connection which assures us that we are not alone."[3] Hagar dialed God's crisis hotline. And God didn't give her immediate deliverance. She wasn't removed from her challenging situation. Instead, the angel told her to return to Sarah, where she would face the same emotions that she had felt before leaving. She would have to deal with her mistress's jealousy and ill will. Her circumstances didn't change, but her outlook did because God saw her. Suddenly she was equipped to move forward because she realized that the God who heard and saw her was also with her.

Whatever your emergency, God is your eternal 9-1-1 operator, always by your side. Take your first measure of comfort in that. Then, throughout your crisis, you can rely on His presence as faithful and true.

God sees you. He hears you, and He knows your need. He knew you even before He fashioned your body inside your mother's womb (Jeremiah 1:5). He is with you in your wilderness.

> *God sees you.*
> *He hears you,*
> *and He knows*
> *your need.*

When Hagar wound up in the wilderness for a second time, child in tow, it had to feel like *déjà vu*. "This again? Really, God?" While the Bible only describes weeping as her response to a second-time wilderness experience, the God who had seen her the first time heard her the second time. And He did the miraculous. He opened her eyes to see water in the wilderness.

The water, what she needed to survive, was available all along; she just hadn't seen it. Did the tears in her eyes block the view of an oasis? Had the sense of being overwhelmed by her circumstances prevented her from seeing the provision God had prepared for her? We don't know from reading the passage. But I know what happens in my heart and life, and I'm guessing it happens to you, too.

I start to feel like God doesn't see me because there is distance between us. Maybe I've been upset over my circumstances, and my anger has separated me from my Heavenly Father. Or perhaps it wasn't anger, but discouragement or worry or fear. These emotions can cloud my vision or block my view too. So while He is the God who sees me, I am the one who can't see Him.

I call this "spiritual separation anxiety." Like a preschooler, I want to step into the classroom without letting go of my daddy's leg first. So when He places me in uncomfortable situations that stretch my faith, I grow afraid and wonder where God is. I forget His promises like, "I will never leave you nor forsake you." Fear grabs hold when my feelings and faith collide.

Choosing our responses at those moments is critical. What if we could pause and, like Hagar, remember El-Roi, the One who sees us? What if we asked God to open our eyes wide to get a glimpse of His preparations and provisions for us? Remembering His promise to hear us when we call would refresh our hearts amid crises.

Even when our eyes are closed, God sees us.

The $5K Drop

Yes, I knew God had placed it on someone's heart to drop five grand in our backyard. I don't bank on that ever happening again, but I never want to forget it. Since I don't have a child to name *Ishmael* ("God Hears"), I did something else to help me remember God's provision in the wilderness: In my home, between the gathering room and kitchen, there's a small partial wall. When I'm standing by the kitchen sink, as I do many times a day, I can see throughout the main floor of the house. Matt hung a word vinyl on that little wall. Any guess what it says?

The angel of the Lord found you in the wilderness.

When desperation strikes and provision is scarce, know that God sees you. He hears you; He knows your need. No prayer is beyond God's reach or reply. There is no prayer too desperate to be heard by Him.

God, See Me

God, help me to trust that You see me. Thank You for being in control and for never leaving me alone. I trust You as my Creator; be my 9-1-1 Operator and Guide. Open my eyes to see Your preparation and provision in this present wilderness.

Chapter One Prayer Principles

- God will not allow your wilderness to go unnoticed.
- Prayer is the strongest weapon in your spiritual arsenal.
- Whatever your emergency, God is your eternal 9-1-1 Operator, always by your side.
- Even when our eyes are closed, God sees us.
- No prayer is beyond God's reach or reply.

CHAPTER TWO

Too Bitter to Swallow

God, Hold Me.

She gasped for breath for four days, and I could barely catch my own through the pain of watching her suffer.

A few weeks before these final moments, I recognized that after twenty-two years of neurological degeneration, Taylor's life had neared its end, but there was no way to fathom just how hard my daughter would battle to keep going. She had fought for each day of her entire life and died the same way, giving it her all.

When Taylor was diagnosed at age four with Sanfilippo syndrome—a rare genetic neurologically degenerative disease—I prayed, "God, heal her. You can do anything. She needs your healing hand. Help us find a cure." For many years, those prayers were on repeat. Treatment was out of reach for this rare genetic disorder, and symptom management seemed the only answer. But even that was a struggle. Between Taylor's limited communication skills and the medication's side effects, managing her symptoms felt like eating chocolate and spaghetti in the same bite.

When God wove her within my womb, Taylor was already genetically missing the ability to produce the metabolic enzymes that everybody needs to grow and function normally. I'm not sure when that reality sank in for me. Some would believe that God created her with imperfections; I'm here to testify otherwise. While Taylor lost her ability to talk, walk, and sing—and eventually couldn't feed herself or even drink from a straw— the way she looked into our eyes displayed love without words: absolute perfection.

One night, not too long after the diagnosis, Taylor fell asleep, and I began to read the latest thesis on treatment for her condition. The theory concluded the most challenging obstacle was the blood-brain barrier. I read for three hours straight to try to understand what this meant. Then, I researched the medical definition for every other word of the theory to understand its meaning. Eventually, I concluded that the "blood vessels in the central nervous system carry unique properties of protection that tightly regulate the movement of ions, molecules, and cells between blood and the brain."[1]

That night, I cried buckets. I wished I were the yelling type so I could scream at God and ask why He created Taylor with what has been called "the Alzheimer's of childhood." But the following day, I began to read where I had left off. Somehow, the night before, I had been focused on the "tightly regulated" portion of the blood-brain barrier's job and missed that it "carried unique properties of protection."

The purpose of the blood-brain barrier is to protect the brain's microenvironment. The barrier that was preventing a cure from reaching the diseased cells in Taylor's brain was also saving it from being attacked by other threatening cells.

The next morning, my prayers shifted from finding a cure to finding courage. If healing were to take place for Taylor on Earth, the journey to reach it would be arduous, and I knew I wasn't up for all the hurdles we'd meet along the way. Who knew that a medical thesis statement would be what God used to whisper to my heart, *I am here for you. I have a bigger plan than you can comprehend, and I'm inviting you on the journey. Will you be bold enough to come along?*

As author Carol Kent says, "When God writes your story, you're in for the adventure of a lifetime." Unfortunately, I could not conjure enough bravery at that moment to face a disease that slowly erased every memory and skill my daughter would ever have. Still, like a little girl who longed to soak up the courage of someone greater than herself, I poured myself out to God and asked Him to keep me as close to Him as possible.

I never stopped praying this prayer, especially during those final four days when Taylor used every ounce of strength to pull oxygen into her lungs and push it out again.

Watching my child suffer while dying is not something I can describe.

The trauma of having an unmarked white van pull into the driveway of our home wrecked this mama's heart and psyche. Seeing my children weep over their sister's body is not something I can unsee. Watching my husband carry her spent body down the stairs her feet had struggled to climb is forever embedded in my memory. Mercy—I couldn't even stand on my own two feet.

I needed to feel God's love wrapped around me in my crumpled state. I could barely repeat the prayer I had learned years earlier: "God, hold me."

Something Desperate

When control eludes our grasp, prayers ascend to fill the gap. If we need provision but don't have it? We're desperate. When we need protection and can't seem to find it? We grow needy before God, for sure. But there are more desperate prayers than the ones we pray in out-of-control situations or in waiting seasons. The depth of despair sinks the farthest when God's answer to our prayers is "No." *No, your loved one didn't make it. No, I'm sorry; the cancer isn't cured. No, your child's diagnosis isn't treatable.*

Our prayers after His answer is "no" become the most desperate requests. "God, why? Where were You? How is this the best result?"

Why doesn't God always answer our prayers the way we want Him to? King David certainly knew a thing or two about this.

From the time he battled the giant to the day he went to the grave, trouble struck David's heart and life, time after time. He was anointed as the next king of Israel as a young man but didn't ascend to the throne for fifteen years—and spent most of that time fighting and running for his life from King Saul. God called David a man after His own heart; yet the Bible tells us he committed heinous crimes—first adultery, and then murder. When he came face to face with the prophet Nathan, David admitted his guilt, but his sin still carried consequences: The child born from his adulterous affair would die.

2 Samuel 12:16 says, "David pleaded with God for the child." Goodness, my mama's heart knows exactly what this feels like. "God, if you'll just (fill in the blank), then I'll (fill in the blank)." And then I personally traded bargaining for begging. "Please, Lord, please." I'm guessing David did the same. As a distraught parent, he fasted and lay on the ground, wrapped in sackcloth, refusing to get up or eat.

Although it is unclear if David wrote Psalm 51 after the death of his baby or before, the introductory words state: "For the director of music. A psalm of David. When the prophet Nathan came to him after David had committed adultery with Bathsheba." The entire psalm is saturated with recollection, repentance, and a request for deliverance. I often wonder if David sang Psalm 51 in a minor key; so great was his sorrow. "Let me hear joy and gladness; let the bones you have crushed rejoice" (Psalm 51:8). David knew the combined weight of regret and grief. Shame and guilt only buried his sorrow more deeply into his heart.

David held a lamenting posture for seven days, until the child died. David's attendants were afraid to tell him what had happened. They thought, "How can we now tell him the child is dead? He may do something desperate" (2 Samuel 12:18).

Something desperate. David was beyond discouraged and depressed. The people who spent the most time with him and knew him better than anyone feared his behavior would worsen upon learning his precious child was dead. Did they worry that he might kill himself—or someone else?

When God doesn't answer our prayers as we want Him to, desperation strikes. We feel as if our bones desiccate into powder, and the simple act of standing becomes more than we can bear. Every breath grows labored. The only way to continue breathing is to remember the Source of oxygen. "In him, we move and live and have our being" (Acts 17:28).

"In him, we move and live and have our being."

From our first breath to our final one, God is the Provider of each one. We rely on our Creator's ability to control the exact amount of oxygen we need each moment of every day, and we must learn to trust that His provision in all things is best for us. But when we've asked for a different set of circumstances or a different outcome than what God gives us, the temptation to try something desperate is natural.

Hold On

The first night after that unmarked van left our home with Taylor's ragged body inside it, Matt and I lay in bed, both feeling the emptiness in the room next to ours, ears strained to hear a cough or sniff where silence now reigned. Then my strong, passionate husband began to weep, and between sobs, I made out his words, "I feel like I'm supposed to go get her." The overwhelming instinct that both of us had to run to the funeral home and scoop her up felt ridiculously impossible to cope with. Everything in my husband said, "Protect your baby girl!" Though his eyes had seen her empty body, his father's heart now saw an empty bed and didn't know what to do.

There were no more words exchanged between us that night. We could only hold each other and weep ourselves into a restless half-sleep.

Rising to the Surface

In 2018, a famous killer whale named Tahlequah birthed a calf that died within a few hours. Orcas are highly social mammals who express many emotions through their habits. Though her baby was not alive, Tahlequah could not let go of her calf; she continually pushed it to the surface of the water for seventeen days—far longer than the average grieving period of a few hours to a day. Marine biologists who tracked the mother's unusual behavior said it's "unprecedented" for an orca to keep this going for so long. Tahlequah traveled more than one thousand miles with the corpse, which had begun to decompose.

"It is a grief, a genuine mourning," said Center for Whale
Research founder Ken Balcomb.[2]

I'm guessing Tahlequah was experiencing the same instinct
that prompted my husband to want to reclaim our daughter's
body from the morgue. Grief drives behaviors we can't rationalize. Sometimes, we can't part with the protective intuitions
God instilled in us. We feel compelled to keep doing what
we've always done, denying the reality of loss.

We all hope for a better outcome than these. Like David,
we desire the miracle. And sometimes, like David—and me and
Matt—we don't receive the answer from God that we longed
for. Then what?

Unanswered Prayers

When our prayers are answered unexpectedly, we are elated. Who
doesn't want God to drop $5,000 in their backyard? But when the
answer is no and the results are not what we had hoped for, human
emotion rises within our hearts and often reigns. We wonder if
God even heard us. We think we must not be worthy of His listening ear. Doubts like, *Maybe I didn't pray long enough or hard
enough*, or *Maybe I just wasn't good enough in God's eyes to
receive the answer I wanted* creep in. These whispers are lies from
the enemy. In Psalm 22:24, David reminds us of what is true:

> For he has not despised or scorned the suffering of the
> afflicted one; he has not hidden his face from him, but has
> listened to his cry for help.

God doesn't tell us "no" out of spite or rejection. It's only because He loves us so much and wants the very best for us that He ever says no. He sees the whole picture from beginning to end; our view is limited.

So many times, we go to God in prayer with predetermined expectations. After all, we know what we want and when we want it. I've never known anyone to pray urgently, "And Lord, it's OK if You don't give it to me right now. Ten years from now would be OK, too." No, many of our requests to God are explicitly tied to our desired timeline. For most of us, that timeline is NOW. The tyranny of the urgent drives our prayers, and desperate prayers are typically rooted in emergencies.

In addition to the moment's rashness, our ideas of how God should respond to our needs dominate our requests. It's not wrong to take our fears, cares, and worries to Him. This is what He tells us to do. "Cast all your anxiety on him because he cares for you" (1 Peter 5:7). We have the promise that He hears us. He listens. "He will respond to the prayer of the destitute; he will not despise their plea" (Psalm 102:17). He always responds—but not always in the way we want.

In urgency, we forget that He still sovereignly rules over the earth. God's plan for our lives is broader than this present moment.

David didn't try to take any drastic measures after his child died. What he did next baffled his attendants; he stopped weeping, wailing, and fasting. He had hoped that his contrition would change God's mind, but when it didn't, he made a statement that ushers hope into my soul:

"But now that he is dead, why should I go on fasting? Can
I bring him back again? I will go to him, but he will not
return to me." (2 Samuel 12:22)

David embraced an eternal perspective, anticipating the day
when he would see his baby in Heaven again, yet stepping into
the life God still had for him to live on this planet right then.

Psalm 51 provides a glimpse into what made David different than his predecessor, King Saul. David repented of his sin,
requested mercy, and loved the Lord so much that he begged,
"Do not cast me from your presence or take your Holy Spirit
from me" (Psalm 51:11). David couldn't live without the Lord,
and with his heart aligned with God's will for his life, he knew
strength for another day would be his. God would hold him.

When we can barely shape the whispered words "God, hold
me" with our lips, what are we really asking Him for? The
same thing David requested. We long for God's presence to
envelop our souls so deeply that it is unexplainable. We want
His peace to calm our hearts and minds, as what Paul promises
in Philippians 4:7 is within our reach: "And the peace of God,
which transcends all understanding, will guard your hearts and
your minds in Christ Jesus." We affirm the pastor's message
when he preaches on this verse. Yes, Lord! Count me in on that
kind of peace.

Shall we back up briefly and check the context for this peace
in the previous verse? Philippians 4:6 says, "Be anxious for
nothing, but in everything, by prayer and petition, with thanksgiving, present your requests to God." Prayer is the prime place

of awareness for the unimaginable peace of God. While we are supposed to present our needs to Him, laying them at His feet, we must always remember that they are requests and not demands. As we approach the throne of almighty God, we know our place and humbly make our case known. God sees our humble hearts, and this posture of humility attracts Him. In our vulnerability, we can release our cares into His arms and enter His incomprehensible peace and presence.

When we ask God to hold us, we also want to know we are not alone in pain, grief, or death. His presence brings comfort, protection, and the knowledge that we cannot walk this journey alone. His omnipresence is not something we can grasp. Where the New International Version of Philippians 4:7 uses the word "transcends" to describe the relationship between peace and understanding, the English Standard Version uses the word "surpasses." In Greek, this word means "to excel, surpass, be superior."[3] God's work in our lives exceeds our ability to comprehend it. His sovereign plan is superior to anything our finite minds can dream up. Believing that our plan is better than God's means believing that we know more than He does.

Hold Me

In some ways, Taylor's last few days felt like a dream. I believe we are closest to sensing the heavenly realm in the first and final moments of our lives. When my babies were born, it was as if Heaven's scent had arrived in our home. But at Taylor's bedside in the final moments of her life, I did not see bright, beautiful lights nor hear angelic singing. I wish that had been my experience. Instead, her ghastly, shallow breathing permitted one last howl, a death moan from the shell of an emaciated body. The hole that moan seared into my heart left a scar. Yet the presence of God blanketed her room, and

> *God was holding her, and God was holding me at the same time, in two different places.*

His Spirit was never more real to me than in that moment.

I felt God wrap His arms around me, and peace overwhelmed my spirit. My prayer for Taylor's healing had been answered. God was holding her, and God was holding me at the same time, in two different places. In my own power, I felt like the crushed bones David describes in Psalm 51, but when I leaned into the Spirit and Word of God, I could rest in the promise that Taylor was now in Heaven. No more seizures. No more vomiting and retching. No jacked-up body that wouldn't work as it should. My precious Taylor would be given a new body to match the beauty of her spirit—one that I can't wait to hug someday.

> *God is big enough to contend with your sorrow. His arms are wide enough to hold you in your pain. Pain cannot grip you tighter than God's grace.*

God is big enough to contend with your sorrow. His

arms are wide enough to hold you in your pain. Pain cannot grip you tighter than God's grace. Those irrational thoughts that invade your mind are not unknown to Him; He can handle whatever emotion you throw at Him. His answer to your prayer is not "no" for denial's sake. Instead, *because* of His mercy, grace, great love for us, and sovereign plan for each of us, He issues "no's" that we can't perceive because we can't predict the future. He can. He will hold you fast and never let go; His love goes beyond the no. His arms are wide enough to hold every broken heart.

When desperation calls, answer in prayer.

God, Hold Me

God, I need to feel Your love wrapped around me. The pain of life is far too agonizing, and my mind can't rationalize my emotions. Blanket my spirit with Your peace and make yourself known to me. For in You, I move and live and have my being. Hold me close, Jesus.

Chapter Two Prayer Principles

- When control eludes our grasp, prayers ascend to fill the gap.
- From our first breath to our final one, God is the Provider of each one.

- God's plan for our lives is broader than this present moment.
- Pain cannot grip you tighter than God's grace.
- When desperation calls, answer in prayer.

CHAPTER THREE

Pain in the Neck

God, Heal Me.

Brains splattered by bullets, infection saturated through flesh into bone, and intestines seeping from an open gut are just a few of the things my husband has seen firsthand that I can't fathom. By the time Taylor was diagnosed, Matt had witnessed twelve years of nightshift debacles in the hospital emergency room. Firsthand observation of the results of accidents and medically volatile situations reinforced his naturally steady nature. One must learn to put boundaries around trauma to respond to it appropriately; Matt is experienced and skilled at this.

But the day we received confirmation of Taylor's diagnosis of Sanfilippo syndrome, Matt read the medical description of the disease and fell on the bed, sobbing. As a medical professional, the impact of the words "average lifespan of ten to fifteen years" struck his heart with intimate sorrow and pain. He wept for the lack of treatment or a cure. He grieved for healing that would never take place. His heart couldn't process the pain his wife and daughter would bear. It was too much for all of us.

Define Healing

Are you wondering how I could be bold enough to pray, "God, heal me," after watching my daughter suffer for twenty-two years and ultimately die? Because, humanly speaking, doesn't death seem like the *opposite* of healing? We logically believe that if someone is dead, it means that God didn't heal him or her. But what I've learned about this desperate prayer of asking God to heal us is that we often don't understand what we are asking for.

The need for healing presents itself in many variations because pain and suffering present themselves in various ways. We pray that God will cure our friend who has been diagnosed with cancer. We long for the Lord to restore a loved one just out of surgery. Anxiety and fear press into our minds, and we ask God to alleviate them. So what is healing?

Is it physical? Yes.

Is it emotional? Yes.

Is it mental?

Is it spiritual? Yes, and yes.

When my kids ask me for something, there's a word they often use: "Mom, I need new shoes." "I really need ice cream." "I need some coffee." Matt and I have grown accustomed to understanding their use of the word "need." We often respond to them by saying, "Define 'need.'" What are we saying to them? *Give us the little details on what you mean by the word "need," because we know you don't really need ice cream, but you might need a new pair of shoes.*

While that analogy feels trivial compared to asking God for healing, sometimes I wonder if when I'm pouring my heart out in prayer, God sees and hears me but whispers, "Define healing." Because my Creator knows what I need so much more than I do.

God's definition of healing and mine may not be the same. From my perspective, healing might be narrowly focused on physical recovery from an illness, emotional relief from pain, or the resolution

God's definition of healing and mine may not be the same.

of a problem. However, God's definition of healing could encompass not only these aspects but also spiritual growth, heart transformation, and alignment with His divine plan.

The Prayer of Jabez

Years ago, God brought *The Prayer of Jabez* by Bruce Wilkinson to my attention,[1] and at the time, it felt to me like everyone and his brother was praying this prayer. Jabez is an anomaly because, amid a long genealogical list of names, the Bible provides a few more details about him than the rest of the people on the list.

> Jabez was more honorable than his brothers. His mother had named him Jabez, saying, "I gave birth to him in pain." Jabez cried to the God of Israel, "Oh, that you would bless me and enlarge my territory! Let your hand be with me, and keep me from harm so that I will be free from pain." And God granted his request. (1 Chronicles 4:9–11)

And that's it. That's all we know about him. Many of the conversations I've read or heard about Jabez emphasize his request for blessing and expansion and presume God's *bada-bing-bada-boom* answer. It seems pretty straightforward, doesn't it? Jabez prayed; God answered. He asked for a blessing, and *boom!*—God gave it. But let's stop and reflect on this passage a little more.

Jabez's name means "sorrowful" or "born of pain." At birth, the poor guy was labeled with "affliction." His mother wanted to ensure he didn't forget how much pain he caused when he was born; she wanted him to carry that reminder to his grave. We don't know the kind of life Jabez had, but whatever his circumstances were, in addition to being called a "pain" from the get-go, we know he craved protection from pain. He followed the pattern of so many of the men and women of the Bible: He cried out to the God of Israel, the One he knew could hear him.

While I can't quote a chapter and verse to support my theory, I believe the blessing and expansion that Jabez prayed for was that his pain wouldn't be wasted. It makes sense that enlarging his territory meant widening the purpose of his pain.

Was his prayer answered readily? If he were in dire pain, did he receive an immediate resolution? This we don't know. The Bible doesn't say what kind of timeline passed upon God's answer to his request. Was it the next day? Ten months? Ten years? We don't have this detail.

Most of us want the blind-man-healed kind of miracle. We lean toward concluding that the relief—or perhaps the prevention—of Jabez's pain flooded in right after God told him to take two Tylenol and go to bed. But I'm not sure it came in the same hour he requested it. If his prayer were for prevention, then that wasn't answered in the moment, either. Dictionary.com defines the noun form of "healing" as "the act or process of regaining health."[2] You see, the healing journey is an invaluable part of becoming healed.

As I mentioned earlier, when we ask God for healing, we usually seek relief from physical, emotional, mental, or spiritual pain or distress. If we desire to heal from physical illness or injury, it's pretty obvious what we are asking for. *Fix my body, God. Make the blind eyes see again; give hearing to the deaf ears. Rid me of cancer or heart disease or sickness. Give me strength to walk again; cure the wounds. Mend the broken places of my human shell.* God is in the physical healing business. Just ask the folks who lined up to be touched by Jesus. More than one hundred Bible verses talk about Jesus's healing people.[3]

But asking God for healing doesn't always mean a request for physical wellness. Many times, we are seeking emotional mending from past traumas or heartbreak. "Lord, let Your Spirit overcome my feelings of disconnection, rejection, or brokenness. Restore me." We long for happiness and joy and crave fulfillment as a natural part of our emotional well-being.

When we pray to God for healing, we want comfort, guidance, and restoration of mind, body, and spirit, believing that He can heal and make us whole again. In a word, healing means "wholeness."

We've established that we want to be healed. But we often prefer a quick fix over a healing journey. We don't really want to be in the healing *process*; we just want the end result. *Make it a done deal. Get over the pain and make it snappy.* Because suffering, to use a word I don't like my kids to say, sucks.

A Holy Privilege

A phone number appeared on the screen, and my heart rate elevated. It was my sister, and I knew the news wouldn't be good.

"Hello?"

"Hey," she said. "What are you doing?"

"Oh, I'm in the store with the girls."

"I promised I would call you if he grew worse. Well . . ." There was a long pause, a deep breath, and then she said, "He's worse."

My dad's skin cancer was nothing new; he'd been receiving treatment for five years. But the top of his head simply wouldn't heal. Blackened flesh surrounded a crater where the diseased tissue had been cut out repeatedly. The cancer had been held at bay but never cured, and now, the specialists and surgeons told our family that the options had run out. It was only a matter of months, perhaps weeks.

When I arrived at my childhood home, my dad was lying in his recliner. My mind's eye flashed back two decades, to a time when my mom had sat in the same place, her body broken by acute myeloid leukemia. The pain in my heart escalated beyond description, and with tears streaming down my face, I kissed my dad on the cheek. He knew who I was, but it was evident that the cancer was winning. That evening, my younger sister and I moved him from the recliner to his bedroom, and I remember doubting that he would ever leave it again.

My sisters and I did our best to keep Dad comfortable throughout the next day—but how do you truly keep your dying loved one "comfortable"? However, Dad had never been a complainer, and he wasn't about to start then. In an effort to distract him, I played hymns on the piano, as all six of his daughters had done for years. When I walked back into the bedroom to check on him, my older sister, Karen, waved for me to continue playing. Dad had been tapping his finger on the bed in rhythm with the music. I returned to the piano and continued playing random pages of the hymnbook until I landed on one of his favorites, "Precious Lord, Take My Hand." Barely making it through one verse and the chorus, I made the song my prayer, begging the Lord to lead my dad home.

Overnight, Dad's breathing slowed and around 10 a.m. the next day, I asked him if I could read the Psalms to him. He could barely speak, but he nodded yes. I sat on the bed, criss-cross applesauce with an open Bible, and began to read Psalm 1 aloud. I paused after a few chapters and skipped over to Dad's favorite psalms—110, 111, and 112—then headed over to my own favorite, Psalm 18. Then I went back to Psalm 4. I tried singing, but that was hideous. My voice just wouldn't hold up through my tears, so I read and commented on the Scriptures, telling Dad if he saw any lights or heard the angels' voices to follow them.

So we had the sweetest worship service together. In many ways, it seemed that time was standing still, yet three and a half hours passed that way. I finally said, "Dad, I'll be right back. I need to call Matt; he'll be worried about me."

I had barely stepped out of the bedroom when my sister, Sharon, called, "Rachel . . ." Hanging up the phone, I rushed back into the room. Dad had graduated to Heaven.

I would have stopped talking much sooner if I had known Dad was waiting for me to hush up before going. He was never one to leave in the middle of a church service. Forty-eight hours had passed since I walked through the door, yet his suffering had made it seem like an eternity. How can a person be so sad to say goodbye and yet so relieved the suffering is over? Dad's healing journey had ended. He's now healed. Past tense. Whole in every possible way, but very far from Earth.

The Fattest Lie about Wounds

Ever heard the saying, "Time heals all wounds"? Yep, me too. And I wanted to punch something when I heard it after all these events, because it's not true. Time doesn't heal all wounds; only God can do that. Hearing that time heals all wounds is incredibly frustrating when a loss brutally wounds you.

But part of this saying is true: Healing requires time.

When we rush to heal, we tend to fail to give ourselves grace. Be gentle with yourself; don't expect a Band-Aid to do the trick. Little

> *Time doesn't heal all wounds; only God can do that.*

by little, healing will take place when you follow the Lord. You may experience a more significant dose of healing at one time through a particular Scripture or the Holy Spirit's speaking to your heart. A worship service or one specific song might significantly speed up your healing. But it could take years to feel fully alive again when you've passed through the pain and suffering this world inflicts. Some issues we experience on this Earth won't see healing while we still live here. How do I know this?

Think about it. Every person Jesus healed while He lived on Earth eventually died. Lazarus experienced death twice! I have imagined what that must have been like for him. I wonder if the second time, he thought, "Oh boy. Here we go again." This world is not permanent. As long as we live on this side of Heaven, we'll face the challenges associated with sin. But that doesn't mean we choose to stop trying to reach wholeness. It

just means we must learn to be patient with the healing process. It doesn't mean we can't embrace the healing God makes
available to us now.

I love receiving emails from readers, but sometimes well-
meaning readers send tough messages. Shortly after my Taylor
girl's death, someone asked: "Why didn't you stand against
(Taylor's fatal report) with faith in God's promises for healing?"

The entire email essentially accused me of lacking faith in
God's promises and power for her to be healed. According to
the writer, I had allowed the enemy to steal Taylor from me
through disease.

First of all, the enemy did not *steal* her. She is in the arms
of Jesus—safe, beautiful, and whole. Satan has no authority
over death or the grave; Jesus paid the penalty for death and
rose from the grave. Hallelujah!

However, the enemy took this well-intended email and
twisted it into half-truths in my head for a while. I pored over
what God's Word says about disease, healing, and purpose. In
my head, I replayed the story of one of the blind men Jesus
healed, detailed in John 9:1–5: The disciples asked Him, "Who
sinned? Who caused this man to be born blind? This man or
his parents?" And Jesus answered, "Neither. He was born this
way so that God's work could be displayed in him."

I believe the person who sent me that email is correct that
God's Word contains promises for healing and that His power
reigns over disease. God is still in the miracle-working, healing
business today because His character has never changed—but
the ultimate healing is heavenly healing. I had to choose to

overlook the strong statements in that email and remember that Taylor's purpose—my purpose—in life is to showcase God's beautiful handiwork.

Why, then, is healing such a process? Why does it take so long?

The Secret to Fast-Track Healing

You know how sometimes you suddenly see something you've never seen in a Bible passage you've read before? One morning, about four months after Taylor's death, I ached with deep sadness and opened my Bible to Isaiah 58. I had little faith that God would speak to me deeply through the passage, especially with a chapter heading like "True Fasting." It seemed far removed from where I was, but I started reading.

In this chapter, Isaiah unfolds a story about the Israelites being mad at God for not seeing their humble hearts while they were fasting. Just absorb that for a minute. They were giving up food to grow closer to God and appeared to want His will for their lives. They desired to know His presence was near them, but it wasn't happening. They asked, "Why have we fasted . . . and you have not seen it? Why have we humbled ourselves and you have not noticed?" (Isaiah 58:3). And God told Isaiah to call them out.

The truth was that they wanted God to hear and answer their prayers. So they checked off the fasting box as part of their formula—but their hearts were far from aligning with His. In essence, they were trying to manipulate Him into answering their prayers by fasting! He told them, "You cannot fast as you do today and expect your voice to be heard on high" (Isaiah 58:4b). Ouch.

The Lord proceeds to tell them what to do instead: Loose the chains of injustice and set the oppressed free. Share your food with the hungry and provide shelter to the needy. Clothe the naked and take care of your own family. And then what will happen? "Then your light will break forth like the dawn, and your healing will quickly appear. . . ." (Isaiah 58:8). Say that again? *Quickly appear.*

YES! Sign me up for that!

As I sat in my sadness with that scripture, God said to my heart, *Do what you can do, and I'll take care of the healing.*

A common misnomer in Christian circles of influence is that we have to be perfectly whole and healed before we can help anyone else. Isaiah 58 tells us the opposite: When we help others amid our pain, we experience healing—and not crock-pot, slow-cooker healing, but Instapot, microwave healing!

How beautiful it is that the Lord's blessings don't stop with the healing. He promises even more:

> then your righteousness will go before you, and the glory
> of the Lord will be your rear guard. Then you will call,
> and the Lord will answer; you will cry for help, and he
> will say: Here am I. (Isaiah 58:8–9)

Remember Jabez's prayer? It makes the most sense to me when we apply his introduction in the Bible before we read the words he prayed: "Jabez was more honorable than his brothers" (1 Chronicles 4:9). I would guess that his obedience, his stretching to follow God at all costs, included the list of to-dos recorded in Isaiah 58. Whether his honor was ministering to his own family or the needy, when Jabez showed up at God's throne, God was ready to listen because the communication channel had long since been established. Jabez was honorable, and he loved God. His God was only ever a call away.

Your cry is heard, and through His Word and His Spirit, God whispers to your heart even today, "Healing is available for you. I am here. My glory is here to protect you." Where pain is found, God's presence abounds.

God, Heal Me

God, I need Your divine hand of healing, whatever You choose for that to look like. Redefine my understanding of wholeness and restore my reliance on You. Preserve my life, protect my spirit, and prevent the pain from overwhelming me. For in Your love and protection, there is freedom. Touch me as only You can.

Chapter Three Prayer Principles
- God's definition of healing and mine may not be the same.

- We often prefer a quick fix over a healing journey.
- Time doesn't heal all wounds; only God can do that.
- When we help others amid our pain, we can experience healing from our pain.
- Where pain is found, God's presence abounds.

CHAPTER FOUR

Help Wanted

God, Help Me.

During the eight months my husband searched for a job in 2021, I prayed daily, "Lord, give us this day our daily bread." The needs of five children don't stop for any reason, and the pressure felt like a dead weight. Financially, our family was in survival mode.

One hot summer day, I was driving home in our 2008 Honda Odyssey, affectionately deemed "Ol' Faithful," when I heard a clank that sank my heart. Pulling off the road, I popped out of the van to see a bolt sticking out of one of the tires. The tire held air, but I knew it had to be repaired immediately. So I crawled back into the van, defeated and turning to prayer, desperate for an answer.

"God, help me. I don't know what to do. I know You are in control and know all about this tire. So I won't fret over how much repairs or a new tire will cost, but I need your help."

Some would think I was silly, praying over a tire. But I didn't know another solution. For decades, I had practiced taking everything to the Lord. There was no money in the bank— no help in sight. Car problems are one of my tipping points; it felt like this was more than I could bear. But I was determined not to let it shove me into despair.

You see, the enemy of our souls likes to push our thoughts toward negativity. If he can make us think that God is against us, he will do it. He wants us to forget that God is good and works all things for our good (Romans 8:28). He does not want us to hold on to the fact that no weapon (including flat tires) formed against us will prosper.

After I got home, Matt and I searched the internet for the tire center closest to the house, then decided that driving slowly there with him following in the other car would be our best option. Although this was the first time we had been to that particular repair center, they told me to bring it over as soon as I could, and they would fit it in. Once we arrived, I stared at the price board in the waiting room, calculating the potential damage and wondering if the credit card we kept for emergencies would be our only option.

Finally, the representative called my name, and when I arrived at the counter, he said, "Good news! We were able to plug and patch the tire, so you don't have to buy a new one." *Oh, thank You, Lord!* I asked for help, and God brought support. Relief washed over my heart, but the repair prices ran across my mind like ticker tape. Meanwhile, the shop clerk printed the invoice, handed it to me, and said, "This one's on us." I stared at it, and the saltiness of tears seeped down the back of my throat.

The invoice balance read $0.00.

Take that, you lousy enemy.

Jehoshaphat's Cry for Help

In 2 Chronicles 20, we read that the people came to Jehoshaphat, king of Judah, with the bad news of a vast army coming against them.

Alarmed, Jehoshaphat resolved to inquire of the Lord, and he proclaimed a fast for all Judah. So the people of Judah came together to seek help from the Lord; indeed, they came from every town in Judah to seek him. (2 Chronicles 20:3–4)

Their situation was a little more dire than a flat tire. Their land was in jeopardy, their homes were at stake, and their families were in danger. So they turned to the Lord in prayer. I love that this is their first response to the situation; what an example for us today!

Let's read Jehoshaphat's entire prayer from 2 Chronicles 20:6–12:

"Lord, the God of our ancestors, are you not the God who is in heaven? You rule over all the kingdoms of the nations. Power and might are in your hand, and no one can withstand you. Our God, did you not drive out the inhabitants of this land before your people Israel and give it forever to the descendants of Abraham your friend? They have lived in it and have built in it a sanctuary for your Name, saying, 'If calamity comes upon us, whether the sword of judgment, or plague or famine, we will stand in your presence before this temple that bears your Name and will cry out to you in our distress, and you will hear us and save us.'

"But now here are men from Ammon, Moab and Mount Seir, whose territory you would not allow Israel to invade when they came from Egypt; so they turned away from them and did not destroy them. See how they are repaying us by coming to drive us out of the possession you gave us as an inheritance. Our God, will you not judge them? For we have no power to face this vast army that is attacking us. *We do not know what to do, but our eyes are on you.*"

It's easy to hone in on the last phrase I emphasized above. Knowing that God is God and that we are not and humbling ourselves before Him is pivotal to prayer, correct? Yes, it surely is. But hang with me for a minute as we mine the nuggets of the king's words in prayer.

A Prayer Pattern Worth Pursuing

The emails I receive from new readers often begin the same way. The introduction will include their name, maybe where they live or what they do for a living, and then abruptly, they will say something like, "Rachel, thank you for your written prayers. I wish I could pray more often, but I don't know what to say." Sometimes words don't feel like enough.

I've found that borrowing the written prayers of others can be a great start to finding my own words of prayer. So whenever I read the prayers of men and women in the Bible, I savor them and even dissect them to learn more. Let's peek at Jehoshaphat's prayer together using a simple acrostic: PRAY.

> *Borrowing the written prayers of others can be a great start to finding my own words of prayer.*

P: Praise God's Power

Jehoshaphat began his prayer by remembering who God is: the One in Heaven, Ruler over the nations, the most powerful God (with a capital G). When we are desperate before the Lord, telling God that we recognize who He is as Creator of the universe provides a pause. It allows our hearts to welcome His divine authority over our human limitations and frailty. I sure can make a mess of things when I think I have circumstances under control. Aren't you thankful that He is God and that we are not? His power is incomprehensible and unmatchable, and when I begin to praise Him for who He is, my heart is reassured of His supernatural ability to help because of the authority He holds over all mankind.

God's omnipotence literally means that His power is unlimited. Jehoshaphat needed power that was outside of his own, and he knew it. He also knew the God who held the power he needed. He was familiar with the behavior of praising God because of the legacy passed down to him from the previous kings, David and Solomon. Check out David's prayer in Psalm 68:28, "Summon your power, God; show us your strength, our God, as you have done before."

R: Remember God's Promises

Jehoshaphat remembered God's promises to the nation of Israel and before that, to His friend, Abraham. It's as if Jehoshaphat was praying, "Remember how You gave this land to us once before, Lord? Remember how much You loved our forefathers?" The Lord loves it when we remind him how He delivered us or others in the past because it fortifies our belief that the future will be no different. His character does not waver. We can rest in the fact that not one of His promises has been broken, and every one of them is true.

Hebrews 6:17 reminds us,

Because God wanted to make the unchanging nature of his purpose very clear to the heirs of what was promised, he confirmed it with an oath. God did this so that, by two unchangeable things in which it is impossible for God to lie, we who have fled to take hold of the hope set before us may be greatly encouraged.

God made a promise and then backed it up with another promise. Isn't that like our God? He not only gives us His word, but secures it by swearing upon His own perfect, eternal, and unchangeable nature. We often forget what God has told us to remember because we are prone to short-term spiritual memory loss or even amnesia. When we pause to remember His promises, our perspective shifts from skeptical to secure.

A: Affirm God's Principles

Jehoshaphat then referred to the prayer King Solomon prayed when dedicating the completed Temple of God. He blessed it as a place where future generations would bow before the Lord in humility, and their cries would be heard.

> "When famine or plague comes to the land, or blight or mildew, locusts or grasshoppers, or when an enemy besieges them in any of their cities, whatever disaster or disease may come, and when a prayer or plea is made by anyone among your people Israel—being aware of the afflictions of their own hearts, and spreading out their hands toward this temple—then hear from heaven, your dwelling place." (1 Kings 8:37–39)

Jehoshaphat knew the prayers of his predecessors, and he also knew the principles of prayer that Solomon had lived by for many years. Those principles included humility and honesty before the Lord. No matter the problems we face, God turns His ear toward the cries of our hearts, and humility especially honors Him.

Y: Yield the Problem

Finally, Jehoshaphat outlined the lack of human power to handle the pending attack. I love that last phrase of his prayer—"We do not know what to do, but our eyes are on You."

Isn't that the crux of "God, help me"? We aren't strong enough, big enough, or wise enough to handle life alone. Our minds can't contain enough knowledge for every problem we face, nor can our hearts hold enough strength to address the issues of this world. We can't google our way to glory. Understanding that God's supernatural power is our best option for success positions us to witness the miracle He wants to perform. As faith hero Corrie Ten Boom explains,

> When we pray, we step inside the room of the general headquarters of God. We may enter through Jesus, who is the Way. Our inability meets God's ability, and then miracles happen.[1]

Are you unsure that miracles still happen today? Ask my friend Danette if they do.

God, Help Me Find My Brother

My friend Danette and I both lost our fathers within a few months of each other. At the small group my husband and I hosted weekly, she shared a prayer request: Her father had left his retirement account to his children, but it was an "all or nothing" situation. Every person listed as an heir had to sign the paperwork before the inheritance could be released. There was only one problem: Danette's brother lived on the city streets and had been estranged from the family for several years. No one knew where he lived, which was the way he wanted it. Our group prayed that he would be found, and we promised to continue praying for Danette and her brother.

Later that week, Danette prayed, "Lord, I can't imagine you would not let our family have this money that my dad worked so hard for and designated to his children. But you are God, and I am not. So I am giving this to You. I don't know where my brother is, but You do. If it is Your will that I find him and we receive this money, I will need Your help." She drove to the area of the city where she had last seen her brother years before, but it was a ghost town. Finally, the Holy Spirit nudged her to stop by a gas station she knew her brother had frequented. She told the cashier, who had only been working there for two months, that she was looking for her brother. The cashier met her gaze and said it just so happened that she was a leader of a missing persons community network.

God had led Danette to the exact person with the expertise to help her find her brother. She gave the cashier all her contact information and then drove home, leaving the situation in God's hands.

The following day, Danette awoke to the sound of her phone ringing. It was her homeless brother. Someone had visited his tent at 3 a.m. and given him a piece of paper with Danette's name and number on it.

The Lord works in mysterious ways, but His promise to help us is alive and well.

The Advantages of Desperation

While crises and moments of hardship don't feel advantageous, they do provide a certain advantage. Our desperate prayers to God in the thick of challenges accomplish things we would not otherwise experience. Pain is often the prompt to prioritize prayer.

First, those situations lead us to admit our fragility. If we look at the words Jehoshaphat prayed before admitting he did not know what to do, we can see the void he was experiencing.

> *Pain is often the prompt to prioritize prayer.*

> "Our God, will you not judge them? For we have no power to face this vast army that is attacking us. We do not know what to do, but our eyes are on you." (2 Chronicles 20:12)

I dare say that 100 percent of our desperate situations leave us feeling powerless. That's why we aren't fond of them. Vulnerability and weakness form a hinge in our souls that can swing either way. When we embrace humility and admit our inabilities, God's ears perk up. It's not that He wasn't listening before, it's just that He recognizes the moment when we are ready to see the actions He's been taking on our behalf. Without bowing in humility before our Creator, we open ourselves to pride and negative emotions that then dictate our actions, often leading to bitterness or rebellion. Our God loves a humble heart, and circumstances beyond our control have a way of ushering in humility.

Secondly, our bottomed-out pleas to God lead us down a path toward deeper communication with Him. From the depths of our most desperate cries for help, we can embark on a journey toward a more profound connection with God. In our everyday lives, we are grateful for a neighbor who gives a pleasant "good morning" wave or thankful for a caring friend who sends a "have a great day" text. But the relationship deepens when we meet them for dinner and enjoy friendly conversation about the most recent book we read or a vacation spot we'd love to visit someday. Then, as we begin to talk about matters of the heart, soul, and mind, the relationship stretches even deeper. We have moved the needle from being acquaintances to friends. Ultimately, when we let our guard down to discuss our weaknesses, we experience the deepest moments in relationships.

If we can picture this journey of friendship with other humans, imagine how much more intimate our Creator longs to be as we talk together. God cherishes our vulnerable moments in conversation with him. His ear is ever listening for our cry, and He is at work on our behalf before we utter a word to Him. Isaiah 65:24 explains, "Before they call I will answer; while they are yet speaking I will hear." God is always only a prayer away. He hears every whisper of your heart and every plea for His mercy. He can't wait to have the next conversation with you.

When Jehoshaphat admitted his hopelessness and helplessness, I imagine God said, "Ahh. He has no idea what I've been working on. Looks like he's ready to glimpse what I'm doing in this situation."

A Single Verse with Long-Lasting Impact

At age four, Taylor could communicate only basic needs and held a limited understanding of what was said to her, but Matt and I never wanted to underestimate her potential. Neither did her Sunday School teacher—so we always took her to class. One Sunday when we went to pick up Taylor, the teacher asked her if she could tell us the Bible verse the class had learned that morning. Proudly, Taylor smiled and announced, "The battle is the Lord's."

The Bible story of David and Goliath from 1 Samuel 17 had been the focus that Sunday. That simple phrase, uttered in Taylor's little voice, echoed in my mind for many years afterward, carrying me over countless challenging hurdles.

After Jehoshaphat admitted that the battle was too large for him and told God he didn't know what to do, a prophet named Jahaziel stepped forward to declare a word from the Lord.

"This is what the Lord says to you: 'Do not be afraid or discouraged because of this vast army. For the battle is not yours, but God's." (2 Chronicles 20:15)

So I echo to you now: Let God be God, because we are not. His help is only a call away. No matter the size of the giant you face, He still slays giants today. You want to be around to see that giant hit the ground.

God, Help Me

God, please help me. I'm sending an SOS to You, Lord, because this battle is too big for me. But I know it's not too big for You. I do not know what to do, so I fix my eyes on You. Father, be my Provider, Protector, and Guide. I need Your help.

Chapter Four Prayer Principles

- Understanding God's supernatural power as our best option for success positions us to witness miracles.
- Our bottomed-out pleas to God lead us on a path of deeper communication with Him.
- When we pause to remember God's promises, our perspective shifts from skeptical to secure.
- Pain is often the prompt to prioritize prayer.
- God still slays giants today. You want to be around to see that giant hit the ground.

CHAPTER FIVE

Chosen and Renamed

God, Reassure Me.

Seventh grade shall forever go down in history as my pitiful year. It was the year of braces, glasses, and ultra-long hair I had no clue how to manage. (You couldn't turn to social media in the 1980s for the latest beauty tips and tricks. In fact, the internet didn't even exist yet.) So imagine the geekiest, most awkward early teen you can; that was me, including the preppy monogrammed sweater to boot. I can laugh now, but it certainly wasn't a joke then.

Three people played a pivotal role in sculpting my self-esteem in my elementary years before I landed in total hormonal teenage chaos. One of them was Betty. Every Sunday when our family went to church, Betty would make a point of talking to me. From the ages of four to six, I remember her saying many times: "Rachel, you have such a pretty smile." Well, gosh, that made it easy to smile at her!

Then there was my dad's good buddy, Bernard. Bernard's jaw-dropping testimony and love for Jesus was contagious. Whenever he saw me, he would smile and say, "Rachel, you just get purtier and purtier." (This was his fun way of saying "prettier.") Of course, he had no idea how much I needed to hear those words. Then again, maybe he did.

The winter of my second-grade year was extra harsh. I still remember how the days dragged by with little daylight and freezing temperatures. For whatever reason, my class's daily reading groups had become a real pain, and whenever my teacher would announce it was time to head to the circular table, all the students would moan and groan, including me. It wasn't the reading I hated; it was the group experience. However, Miss Manning had a way of drawing out the best in me; she began calling me "Sunshine."

My little seven-year-old heart wanted to live up to that name.

Fast-forward thirty years, to the moment when I was scribbling a journal entry about God's calling me to speak and write for Him. My first traditionally published book, *One More Step: Finding Strength When You Feel Like Giving Up*, hit the shelves a few years later. God had allowed me to walk out His calling on my life.

But eight more challenging years would pass before I finally signed a contract to produce the work you're reading now. I could hardly wait to let people know of God's goodness. I posted a smiling selfie across all my social media channels to share the big news. Many wonderful friends sent their congratulations via text, email, and direct messages; it was such an incredible moment of celebration.

But one comment especially stood out to me. It was from Miss Manning, my second-grade teacher, and it simply read: "Congratulations, Sunshine."

A Name Change

Genesis 12 tells us that the Lord told a man named Abram to leave his father's country and move to a new land, a place he'd never been to before. He also promised to make Abram's future family into a great nation and a blessing to all the people of the earth. Genesis 12:4 says, "So Abram went, as the Lord told him. . . ." No questions asked; no push-back on God's command. Abram simply obeyed.

Some time later, God approached Abram in a vision and said: "Do not be afraid, Abram. I am your shield, your very great reward" (Genesis 15:1). This time, though, Abram asked God a question: "What can you give me since I remain childless?"

That's a profound question. Would you agree that if Abram was destined to become the father of a great nation, he had to start by becoming the parent of at least one child? Can you blame him for asking God that question? I can't. It's the same thing we do today when life isn't going exactly the way we thought it would. Our confidence in prayer often declines when we struggle to see how God is working through our circumstances. Naturally, we start asking Him questions.

In the next moment, God took Abram outside and showed him the stars.

> "How high can you count, Abram? You can't finish counting the stars. So your children will be more than you can number."
>
> Abram believed the Lord, and he credited it to him as righteousness. (Genesis 15:7)

This is the stopping point in most sermons or teachings on this passage. Many times, I've paused to admire Abram's faith at this seeming conclusion, but God didn't stop there. He reminded Abram that another reason He had led him that far in the journey was to give him the land he was standing on.

Once again, Abram asked, "How can I know I will gain possession?" You can't blame him for asking a second question, either; at that point, nothing God had promised him had come to fruition except the promise to guide him on his way. Abram had to ponder how he would obtain blessings he could see with his eyes and touch with his hands when nothing was happening naturally. Yet once again, God affirmed His promise.

I often wonder if Abram's prayers of questioning God were recorded in the Bible so we can be assured that it's OK to go to Him with our own questions. He's more than large enough to handle them. His promises do not depend on our ability to understand them. God's principles gracefully go beyond the grasp of our comprehension. Praise the Lord for that.

But years passed, and God still had not provided Abram with what He had promised. Abram was seventy-five, and his wife, Sarai, was sixty-five; the time for having children seemed to have been exhausted, and all hope was gone.

> His promises do not depend on our ability to understand them.

Abram was ninety-nine years old when God appeared to him yet again with the same announcement: "I've promised you that if you are faithful, I will keep my covenant and increase your family." But that time, He added a new element to the equation; he changed Abram's name to Abraham and Sarai's to Sarah.

What's the significance of those few letters? The "ah"—the breath of God was now upon their very names. No longer would Abram be an "exalted father" whose heritage rested on the laurels of his earthly family; the name "Abram" looked to the past for its definition. But Abra*h*am—"father of a multitude"—was a prophetic nod to the beautiful future God had promised to give him. God saw Abraham for who He had called him to be, so He began to call him as He saw him. The perfect verbal form of Abram's name, "Abraham," is used here repetitively to emphasize God's intention.[1] Abraham had asked for reassurance, and God delivered. No longer would he be defined by the past, but his new name would forever be a reminder of God's promises. Abraham wasn't the only one whose name was changed; God also gave one to Sarai: Sar*ah* indicated she would be not only a mom to one, but the mother of many.

Imagine ninety-year-old Sarah's comical expression each time she corrected her name from "Grandma" to "Mom" when people saw her with her precious little one, Isaac, years later. I'm guessing Abraham grinned back at her and then winked. God always provides what He promises.

An Adoption Story

Just before Thanksgiving in 2018, Matt and I knew that Taylor's health was failing—and picking up speed. Her seizures had become more frequent and even more challenging to control with medication. The neurotransmitters in her brain began to run out of undamaged places through which to route their signals, and chaos ensued. One evening, with tear-filled eyes, Matt told me he wished he had adopted her.

Matt's story with Taylor had begun twenty years earlier. She was enamored with Matt from the day I took her to meet him and his daughter, Tiffany, at the zoo in 1999 when we were still dating. She was only four at the time, and in my rush to leave the house, I had forgotten to bring a stroller. So Matt carried Taylor most of that first day. She had no objections and melted in his arms, enjoying the feelings of security and safety.

I can't explain what happened to Taylor's relationship with her biological father. While it began strongly, with him committing to spend time with her after our divorce, circumstances changed over the years, and gradually, the relationship faded. His visits became fewer, but Taylor's declining brain still needed the familiarity of a face and routine to maintain strong recognition. Taylor last saw her biological father when she was eleven; when she turned eighteen, he signed all his guardianship rights over to me. But Matt had always wanted to honor Taylor's father by allowing him to care for her, so he had never tried to formally adopt her.

"Daddy Matt," as Taylor affectionately called Matt before she lost her ability to speak, had cared for her for nineteen years when he told me he wished he'd given her his name. His idea of fatherhood had nothing to do with blood and everything to do with emulating his Heavenly Father. He had chased Taylor in ballparks, carried her on trips, cleaned up her messes, and cared for her every need. His love for her was unconditional, and his heart is bigger than the moon.

When I saw the wistful look in Matt's eye, I knew we had to try to complete the adoption. So we filed the paperwork, not knowing just how ill Taylor would quickly become.

Three weeks later, Taylor landed in the hospital. I called the probate court to expedite the adoption. In typical Taylor fashion, somehow she pulled out of that funk, and miraculously, I drove her home from the hospital on December 18, 2018.

But we hadn't been home long when we realized that her rebound was temporary. I could tell from her symptoms that Taylor would leave us for Heaven very soon, and I was afraid to hope that the adoption would be finalized before then. Matt and I paid money we didn't have to expedite the process and called for legal help. We prayed for the Lord to sustain Taylor until Matt could make her his own by giving her his last name.

Through unbelievable timing, the guardian *ad litem* assigned to our case visited our home on December 29 and completed her report over the weekend. She submitted it to the court the following Monday morning, and at noon, we received a phone call that the magistrate was willing to hold an adoption hearing at 2 p.m. on New Year's Eve. (Who knew the courthouse was even open on New Year's Eve?!) It felt like we were all in another world, or a movie or TV show. The kids piled into the van, Matt drove over from work, and the whole crew scrambled to the courthouse—including two of my sisters who had just "happened" to be visiting from out of town. (God is extraordinary in the way He handles the details!)

Just before leaving Taylor with the nurse at the house, I whispered in her ear that we would be back. Daddy had some big news he would share with her when he got home. I asked her to hold on for us until the hearing was over and we could get back. "It won't take long," I promised. I hadn't left the house often in days, fearing she would die while I was not with her.

When Taylor was six years old, she wore an oversized "sister" shirt for the first time after her brother Michael was born. I'll never forget the day she stood over his hospital baby bed and said one of her last complete sentences: "This is Michael. I'm a big sister."

But now, our family was standing in a courtroom without her. Michael—her "little" baby brother—stood tall beside the robed magistrate and declared, "Yes, Taylor's my sister." Matt affirmed his father's love for Taylor to the judge. Then she passed Michael the gavel, and he pounded it as she declared two incredible words:

"Adoption granted."

Miraculously, our Taylor legally became Taylor Wojnarowski, daughter of Matthew and Rachel Wojnarowski.

She received her new name just two days before Heaven called her home.

Where's My Miracle?

Bible scholars aren't sure who wrote the book of Hebrews—but whoever it was, I sincerely appreciate the person who shared beautiful insight into the life of Abraham. Hebrews 6 explains the certainty of God's covenant with Abraham: God swore on Himself that He would keep His promise to make Abraham a nation, and the following passage explains why.

> People swear by someone greater than themselves, and the oath confirms what is said and puts an end to all arguments. Because God wanted to make the unchanging nature of his purpose very clear to the heirs of what was promised, he confirmed it with an oath. God did this so that, by two unchangeable things in which it is impossible for God to lie, we who have fled to take hold of the hope set before us may be greatly encouraged. We have this hope as an anchor for the soul, firm and secure. (Hebrews 6:13–19)

God changed Abram's name to Abraham when he was ninety-nine years old. A year later, He gave Abraham and Sarah Isaac, the son they had longed for, when Abraham turned a hundred years old and Sarah was ninety. One phrase that arrested me in this passage is "after waiting patiently." Yes, indeed! Do you think Abraham might have been just a little desperate by then? Yet, even though we know he and Sarah made at least one attempt to usher in God's blessings through their own under-standing—remember that debacle with Hagar and the son she conceived with Abram, Ishmael?—God still gives them credit for being patient. What grace!

In Hebrews 11, the Bible's famous "Hall of Faith" chapter, the writer gives Abraham and Sarah some major faith credit with nine verses explaining their story, more than any other hero on the list. I've always found it fascinating that the writer describes Abraham there as being "as good as dead." Isaac was a miracle for many reasons. First, God not only had to reverse the aging process of Abraham and Sarah's bodies; they also had to conceive. And then there was the miracle of carrying that precious baby to full term, when so many things can go wrong with geriatric pregnancies. Thirdly, don't forget the miracle it took to deliver that sweet baby!

If you're enduring life struggles right now and wondering why it doesn't feel like your miracle is coming, Abraham and Sarah surely felt your pain. If your questions to God sound something like, "Ummm, God, do You need a little help here?" then you aren't the first person to think that way. Abraham and Sarah's long wait included a gamut of emotions. I think that's why I smile at that description of Abraham being "as good as dead." He was a goner in every possible way, emptied of his strength and energy and fresh out of potential and ideas. When it seemed like all viable options had been exhausted, God said, "They're ready for the miracle of a lifetime now."

Maybe you are feeling guilty for questioning God the way Abraham did. That last-minute prayer you threw up when you asked if He could use your help brings shame to your heart now. While we know God, our Creator, doesn't need our pitiful human help, we forget that He loves us so much that He would rather hear about our hurts than not hear from us at all.[2]

Sometimes we get prayer so wrong. We've been given all the models and taught all the methodology—at least, I have. The idea of following prayer patterns translates into thinking we have to get it

> **Perhaps desperate prayers are the perfect prayers.**

"right." I enjoy a good prayer pattern, but in our picture-perfect culture, we try to perfect even our prayer lives to our own detriment. By contrast, the psalmist raggedly begged God,

> Listen to my cry, for I am in desperate need; rescue me from those who pursue me, for they are too strong for me. Set me free from my prison, that I may praise your name. (Psalm 142:6–7)

Perhaps desperate prayers are the perfect prayers.

Living It Out

We live in a world that believes all's well that ends well. Happy Hallmark endings rev some people up; our favorite stories end with the hero at the helm. But the miracle of Isaac didn't end at his birth, and the tests to Abraham's faith didn't end at age one hundred. Genesis 22 tells us, "Some time later God tested Abraham"—again.

Couldn't enough be enough? No. God still had some reassurance to give, and Abraham's faith continued to have room to grow. The test consisted of Abraham being willing to travel where God told him to go. No problem; Abraham already had a lot of practice in that department.

> By faith Abraham, when called to go to a place he would
> later receive as his inheritance, obeyed and went, even though
> he did not know where he was going. (Hebrews 11:8)

But then God told Abraham to sacrifice Isaac once he arrived at that place. Whoa—that was an entirely different matter! When Isaac reminded Abraham not to forget the lamb for the sacrifice they were to make to the Lord when they reached their destination, Abraham replied that God would provide the lamb Himself.

The one who had been "as good as dead" reasoned that God could even raise the dead (Hebrews 11:19). Why? He had experienced a miracle in his own life, family, mind, and body. He refused to rely only on what he could see and touch and was determined to rely on the awesome power of his God and who he knew Him to be. Abraham knew God's covenant with him was as accurate as His name because God was the One who had changed his name. From an "exalted father" to the "father of multitudes," Abraham's honest and vulnerable conversations with God ushered in an intimate relationship that didn't falter in impossible situations.

Circumstances have zero effect on God's character. Hallelujah for that.

After the Fact

Two weeks after we buried our precious Taylor girl, I grabbed the mail after the other kids came home from school one day. I opened an official-looking envelope from the state, and instantaneous tears flooded my cheeks. I never knew that when an adoption is completed, the original birth certificate is reissued. The government replaced Taylor's birth certificate, officially listing Matt as her father as if he had been present the moment she was born.

Before taking her last breaths, our hard-fighting Taylor girl stepped into the name she always had worn in the spirit. You see, "Wojnarowski" means "warrior." Taylor, whose battle was forever the Lord's, became Taylor the Warrior.

Adoption is a phenomenal picture of God's redemptive grace. God loves you so much that the day you accept Christ, He adopts you into His family. Your record of being born into sin is erased, and your spiritual birth certificate lists your Heavenly Father's name. You are now a child of the Most High King.

In desperate moments of prayer, when it feels like you have been abandoned or neglected, know that your circumstances can never be too big for God's presence and comfort to fill. His timing will be perfect because He loves you too much for anything less. He named you, and when He sees you, He sees who He created you to be—nothing less. As His child, you can be confident that God sees your potential from before the womb.

God, Reassure Me

God, I can't see Your work in this situation, and I'm tempted to ask if You need my help. Lead me to remember that You see me for who You called me to be. Open my eyes to see You for Who You are: the God of the universe, Who calls me His child.

Chapter Five Prayer Principles

- God's principles do not rely on our ability to understand them.
- God sees you for who He called you to be.
- God always provides what He promises.
- Perhaps desperate prayers are the perfect prayers.
- Circumstances have zero effect on God's character.

CHAPTER SIX

Limps and Scars
God, Protect Me.

Darkness fell, and in the same way most mothers pause after tucking their young children into bed for the night, I, too, would sigh a sweet thanks to God for the gift of another day and the little blessings I called mine. But for the first ten years of our marriage, a couple of hours after the kids' bedtime, Matt would leave to work at the hospital overnight. While I tried to bid him good night with love and care, I didn't want him to go at all.

After he left and I lay in bed alone, my anxious mind raced. *What if there is a fire? How will I ever get these babies out safely? What if my Taylor girl has a seizure? What if she stops breathing? What will I do if anyone gets sick?* So many fear-filled questions bombarded my mind that sleep would not come. With no relatives living nearby, it was just me. And God.

Facing Fear

While I've often heard that the words "fear not" or "don't be afraid" occur 365 times in the Bible, I've never been able to find full proof of this exact number as a fact. However, I have been able to verify that the message that God does not want us to be afraid is repeated many times throughout both the Old and New Testaments. The children of Israel were often told to "be strong and courageous" and even to "be strong and very courageous." Jesus specifically told the disciples not to fear when they were panic-stricken. Why is fear such a battle for humanity if God doesn't want us to be afraid? Why does fear prevent us from praying in life's darkest moments?

Fear prompts an automatic response to keep us safe. Sometimes, that means we kick into fight mode. Other times, fleeing from danger seems like the better choice. Then there's the freeze response we have when fear paralyzes us, rendering us unable to speak or make any decision. Psychologists have labeled a fourth potential response to fear as "fawning," when we try to combat alarm by appeasing the party we feel is in control of the situation.

Enter Jacob, an Old Testament patriarch who tried all those responses to fear at various times. The first thing he did was flee from his childhood home to save his own life—a classic fear response! (He had stolen his older brother's birthright at his mother's behest. I know, it's like a modern-day reality TV show!) He wound up living with his uncle, Laban, in a far-off country, where he tended his flocks, married his daughters, and started a family and business. But after over fourteen years of settling in, marrying, and working for his father-in-law while developing his own sheep herding business, he felt compelled to return to his homeland. In that, he faced an even bigger dilemma: facing the older brother who had previously declared his intention to kill him. So, in Genesis 32:7, we find Jacob "in great fear and distress."

Jacob reacted to this fear in three ways:

1. He divided his family and all the people with him into two camps, reasoning that if Esau attacked one, the other might escape. (A wise, strategic decision.)
2. He prayed. (A faith response—and possibly a desperate prayer.)
3. He selected a gift for Esau and sent his servants ahead of his family with detailed instructions on how to deliver it. (His "fawn" response.)

We don't have a clear, healthy example to follow in Jacob's life journey. This wasn't the first time he tried to bribe, connive, or worm his way out of a problem (the name "Jacob" actually means "heel-catcher," and indicated that he struggled with a tendency to be cunning and somewhat deceitful throughout his early life). However, he did get something right—he prayed.

> "O God of my father Abraham, God of my father Isaac, Lord, you who said to me, 'Go back to your country and your relatives, and I will make you prosper,' I am unworthy of all the kindness and faithfulness you have shown your servant. I had only my staff when I crossed this Jordan, but now I have become two camps. Save me, I pray, from the hand of my brother Esau, for I am afraid he will come and attack me, and also the mothers with their children. But you have said, 'I will surely make you prosper and will make your descendants like the sand of the sea, which cannot be counted.'" (Genesis 32:9–12)

Jacob acknowledged that all his blessings came from the Lord and readily admitted his own unworthiness. His prayer makes me chuckle a little. His humility is touching, but he also said he was afraid he would be attacked and followed up with this: "Oh yeah, and Lord, don't forget the mothers and children." His first thought was, "Save me!" So essentially, his prayer was three words: "Lord, protect me."

Fear, Worry, and Anxiety, Oh My!

The Merck Manual, a leading professional guide for medical and psychological teams, lists more than five hundred phobias that humans can encounter.[1] Until recently, medical and psychological professionals maintained that anxiety and fear are entirely different emotions, saying anxiety is prompted by "uncertain threats" (thoughts or images in our minds), while concrete threats of imminent events that we have or will soon experience with our senses cause distress. But in 2020, the *Journal of Neuroscience* published research that indicates anxiety and worry are not processed in different places in the brain, as previously believed, but that they share a network.[2] Therefore, our emotional responses are natural whether the threats are internally or externally experienced.

I didn't have any visible proof of immediate danger when Matt left home for work each night all those years ago. But the fear that gripped my heart when I would lie down to sleep was as real as if a snake was lying under my bed. I knew something had to change. None of the typical fear responses served me well, and I tried all of them. I tried to bury my head in the pillow and forget about the fears and worries of being alone with the children if an emergency struck. I tried counting sheep. (Whoever came up with that?) I needed so much more: I needed the Good Shepherd.

I started by printing scriptures on cards that I tucked into my nightstand drawer and reading them before turning out the light. Then, I would pray while sitting on the side of the bed, asking God to ease the tension in my back and neck, reminding Him that I believed He was with me. Mostly, my prayer echoed Jacob's: I asked Him for protection.

Throughout that season of Matt's working the night shift, my journey of combating fear was sometimes two steps forward and three steps back, but I was determined not to let fear reign over my heart.

Once during this time, my son had an allergic reaction, and I called 9-1-1 in the middle of the night. But by the time paramedics arrived at our door, the Benadryl had kicked in, and Samuel was sleeping soundly without struggling for breath. Another time, I heard a noise in the basement and wondered if maybe an animal or even a human had made its way in. So I again called 9-1-1, apologizing to the firefighters for my alarm and thanking them for their gracious investigation.

I would sleep, then wake in the wee hours of the morning and struggle to fall back asleep. I didn't want to turn on the light in the middle of the night in order to read Scripture because the light would only cause me to become more alert. So I began to read a curated group of verses from my blog before bed. Then I would tuck my Bible under my pillow, literally resting on God's Word. If I woke up in the middle of the night, I'd stretch my hand underneath the pillow, feel my Bible, and whisper a short prayer. It was often simply, "Lord, protect the children and me." By consistently giving Him my concern, worry, and angst, I began to claim victory over them.

One of the passages I claimed continually was 1 John 4:18: "There is no fear in love. But perfect love drives out fear, because fear has to do with punishment. The one who fears is not made perfect in love."

Intense fear no longer keeps me awake at night. What a

> *Consistent prayer promotes victorious prayer.*

sweet reward it was to experience freedom from that wild ride! And just about the time that I finally learned to rest in God's protection, He answered our prayers for Matt to work the day shift. Consistent prayer promotes victorious prayer.

What Keeps You Up at Night?

Your spouse may not work the graveyard shift like mine did, but I'm guessing something in your life has challenged your sleep or ushered fear into your heart. When she was about four, my youngest daughter, Tessa, had many fears. Each night when Matt would pray with the children individually, Tessa's prayer list (which her sisters still remember!) included asking God for protection from "doggies, wolves, pictures on the fence, giant babies, bugs, chips, lamby, lice, waves, and turbo." While your list may not look like hers, we all have fears. And we all have reactions to those fears.

After Jacob prayed for God to protect him from Esau, he reacted by fawning. Looking over all he had brought on his journey, he selected presents for his servants to take to his brother. He hoped to appease Esau with the gifts so he would receive him well and not attack his family. Check out Genesis 32:21: "So Jacob's gifts went on ahead of him, but he spent the night in the camp."

However, sleep would not come. The next verse explains that Jacob got up in the middle of the night, woke up his entire family, and sent them across the river with all his possessions. This doesn't seem very strategic, but I'm guessing it was his 9-1-1 moment. Don't you wonder if his family complained?

The Bible doesn't say what prompted Jacob to do this; maybe he heard leaves blowing in the breeze and thought, *What if that's Esau coming to hunt me down?* Apprehension of some kind propelled him to get out of bed and move everyone across the river.

Whatever the rationale, or lack thereof, crossing the river sounded simple, but it most likely wasn't. BibleAtlas.org explains,

> The bed of the (Jabbok) river is in a deep gorge with steep, and in many places precipitous, banks. It is a great cleft, cutting the land of Gilead in two. . . . The length of the stream, taking no account of its innumerable windings, is about sixty miles. The mouth of the river has changed its position from time to time. . . . The river is fordable at many points, save when in full flood.[3]

Jacob had to find a fordable crossing on a dangerous river in the dark for a multitude of people and animals. Adrenaline must have played a part in his decision-making process.

Then, once Jacob was left alone on the river's edge, a man came and began to wrestle with him. During the struggle, he touched Jacob's hip, wrenching it out of its socket. However, Jacob was not about to give in and demanded a blessing from the man. The man then changed Jacob's name to "Israel," which means "he who struggles with God." When he realized Jacob would not let go, he blessed him and disappeared.

Afterward, Jacob realized he had wrestled either with God or an angel of God (some scholars believe it was the preincarnate Christ). So he named the place "Peniel," which means "face of God," because he had seen God face to face and lived.

Wow, what a story to share with the children and grand-children! This would have been a match to brag about—one that could have gone down in the wrestling books. But although Jacob received the blessing he was begging for, he also walked away with a limp—something he hadn't asked for. Both the blessing and the limp resulted from what kept Jacob up that night.

Maybe you're saying, "If this is what God's protection looks like, I don't want to pray for it!" Many theologians believe the limp remained with Jacob for the rest of his life. Hebrews 11:21 tells us, "By faith Jacob, when he was dying, blessed each of Joseph's sons, and worshiped as he leaned on the top of his staff." It is assumed that he had to lean on the staff to worship because of his limp. Dr. Tony Evans explains, "It's as if out of all the colorful scenes in Jacob's life, the writer of Hebrews wanted to say, 'In the end, Jacob was a man who was forced to lean on God.'"[4]

Sometimes, God's protection looks like giving us a limp. Jacob had gripped God's shoulders and looked Him in the eye, appealing for His blessing. While God gave it, He didn't want Jacob to forget the experience—but even more than that, He didn't want him to forget that total dependence on God provides the most excellent protection from God.

The enemy doesn't want to be near God. He doesn't want to be near anything or anyone who is near God. The limp was an invitation for Jacob to rest in the arms of his Savior and allow God to protect him from the enemy. Without that limp, the temptation to run on his own and leave God's protection behind would have been too much for Jacob to handle.

The Ultimate Wrestling Match

Like Jacob, I've wrestled with God over scary circumstances. I've even challenged the Almighty because suffering came to visit me and overstayed her welcome. To be truthful, she was not welcome at all.

One spring day in 2017, I stood by the window in Taylor's bedroom, looking out at the sky just after she had experienced a grand mal seizure. After watching her entire body shake and churn as her uncontrolled eyes rolled, and praying for God's peace to blanket her, the seizing finally stopped and she lay on the bed, exhausted. What seemed like an eternity had lasted only fifteen to twenty seconds. Wrung out like a rag doll, Taylor began to fall asleep, and I had a few words with God. Momma Bear was riled! The conversation swelled to a wrestling match of epic proportions as I angrily cried out, "God, You don't know! You don't know what it's like to watch Your child suffer and die!" I didn't think I could stand much more.

While I've never heard God audibly, I heard Him speak directly to my heart in that moment.

"Oh yes, I do. I sent My Son to suffer and die for you."

It was so clear that it captured my breath. It wasn't a thought I could conjure up on my own, especially not at the emotional height of that moment. Frozen in place, I stared at the sky and wondered how God had been able to do that. How did He love the whole world so much that He gave His one and only Son? Unlike Taylor's condition and its painful results, which just *happened*, everything about the long, drawn-out torture and suffering Jesus experienced in the long hours before His death on the cross had been *planned* since before the beginning of time. Willingly. The Father knew it was going to come, what that would feel like, what that would cost Him—and did it anyway.

From this experience, I fully understood that perfect love throws aside fear, anxiety, and worry, and prayer is the first step to embracing God's perfect love. Then He answers our intimate demands for understanding with a blessing that might include the wrenching of a hip, resulting in a limp. In other words, God uses some issues in this world to keep us close to Him for our good—His protection in action.

I can honestly say that my sweet girl, Taylor, and her fight with disease kept me tethered to Jesus. Part of my angst after she left us for her heavenly home is every grieving parent's fear: that people would forget her. That they would forget her beauty, cour-

> *God uses some issues in this world to keep us close to Him for our good— His protection in action.*

age, and strength. They would forget her sparkle, joy, and incredible way of making people smile. I even worried that I, over time, might forget all the struggles and think I could make it through my days without the Lord's moment-by-moment guidance. But I've discovered that when one journey's struggles end, new ones often begin. This is God's merciful protection of keeping me from self-sabotage or self-destruction.

When Taylor was born, I required an emergency C-section. Afterward, one of the things the doctor was proud to tell me was that even though it was an emergency (only eight minutes passed from the surgery decision moment to Taylor's delivery!), she was able to make a small incision that wouldn't be seen. Scarring would be minimal. It was easy to see that this gave her joy as a surgeon. I smiled, but I didn't think much about it after that. Only after Taylor's death would I would find joy in that scar: It was a permanent mark on my body, what some would consider ugly or imperfect, that I now see as a beautiful reminder of God's protection. Staying as close to Him as possible is how I long to live.

Whatever keeps you awake at night is what God wants to use to move you closer to Him. No fear is too great or small for Him to guard you against. The more aware you are of God's presence, the stronger you'll feel His protection.

God, Protect Me

God, I'm afraid. I need Your blessing and protection. Please help me to rely entirely and fully on You as my Defender. May my limp remind me to lean wholly on You for strength and guidance. May my scar be a reminder of Your preservation.

Chapter Six Prayer Principles

- Consistent prayer leads to victorious prayer.
- Sometimes, God's protection looks like a limp.
- Perfect love throws aside fear, anxiety, and worry; prayer is the first step to embracing His perfect love.
- Whatever keeps you awake at night is what God wants to use to move you closer to Him.
- The more aware you are of God's presence, the stronger you'll feel His protection.

CHAPTER SEVEN

Directionally Challenged

God, Guide Me.

"Wake up early, wake up early, wake up early . . ." I had whispered to myself as I fell asleep, but the next thing I heard was Mom's voice saying, "Get dressed; it's time to go!" I could hardly wait to see the ocean, which seemed incredibly far from the Appalachian woods to six-year-old me.

Lucky enough to land on the front row of our family's twelve-passenger van that time, I sat just behind my dad, who was in the driver's seat. I leaned forward to stick my head between the edge of his seat and the seatbelt to feel the air blowing back from the rolled-down window, the only AC available. When I grew tired of the noise in my ears, I settled into studying the magic of the *Rand McNally Atlas*. It was the best way to know precisely how to get to Myrtle Beach, South Carolina, from Richwood, West Virginia, and after thirty minutes, I dared ask the proverbial question:

"How much farther?"

To which my father replied, "We're closer than we've ever been."

I have no idea how many more times I asked the question over the next ten hours, but I know it was a lot. Each time, he echoed, "We're closer than we've ever been."

No Easy Task

Abraham's servant, Eliezer, was accustomed to hard work. As the senior manager of the entire household, he shouldered every responsibility with care. But choosing a wife for Isaac? Really, Abraham? How could he possibly know which woman would suit his master's son? Abraham's instructions didn't come with a *Rand McNally Atlas* but included specific travel directions: The woman to be Isaac's bride could not come from the neighborhood, but from Abraham's native country. She needed to have roots within his bloodline.

Genesis 25:1–4 explains:

Abraham was now very old, and the Lord had blessed him in every way. He told the senior servant in his household, the one in charge of all he had, "Put your hand under my thigh. I want you to swear by the Lord, the God of heaven and the God of earth, that you will not get a wife for my son from the daughters of the Canaanites, among whom I am living, but will go to my country and my own relatives and get a wife for my son Isaac there."

Abraham took his responsibility to his future grandchildren so seriously that he required his servant to swear an oath that he would do precisely as he was bidden. If the tent walls had had ears, they would have heard, "Eliezer, I'm trusting you. Don't let me down."

But exactly how to execute that plan required more logic. "What if the woman I choose won't come with me?" Eliezer asked. "Should I take Isaac to meet her instead?" Abraham nixed this idea entirely and promised that an angel of God would go before Eliezer to help him. But if the woman refused to return with him, Eliezer would be released from the oath he'd sworn.

So the faithful servant loaded ten camels with gifts and set out on the journey. When evening arrived, he stopped at a well, and the camels knelt to rest. He had obeyed his master's direction until he could walk no further. He had exhausted the general instructions. What next?

A Sermon Illustration I Never Forgot

Numbness on my backside always reminds me of sitting through long church services on pad-less pews. Because my father was committed to attending church on Sunday morning, Sunday night, and Wednesday night every week, I had already sat through a lot of preaching by the age of four. I enjoyed the stories tucked into the pastor's messages and took special notice of his sermon illustrations, especially the ones I could picture in my mind's eye.

One Sunday night, the pastor shared how he had recently jumped in the car to go to the store. He said he didn't think about the time of day or worry that a blanket of thick winter darkness would be settling over our small town by the time he finished shopping. He didn't get upset that it was dark when he left the store, and he didn't refuse to turn on his headlights on the way home and then get anxious that he could see only a few yards ahead. He could have gotten angry and shaken his fist at the car, screaming, "Why don't you show me all the way home?" But of course, he didn't. And yes, it would have looked quite absurd if he had.

He simply got in the car and began to drive home. As he progressed, the headlights revealed the road little by little; he saw as far ahead as he needed to in order to make it there safely. The light was sufficient—but he still had to get in the car and move.

Many of us tell God we trust Him. We tell Him we love Him and want to follow His plan. We whisper in prayer that we need His guidance, but truthfully, we want the headlights to shine on every patch of our path from here all the way to Heaven. We want God to reveal His entire plan for our lives in one fell swoop. *Bird's-eye view with a side of GPS, please. And* stat.

But Eliezer's example shows us that obedience in following what we already know from God's principles and promises is the first step of general guidance and direction. Like a compass, God uses His Word, His Spirit, and His people in tandem to guide us.

We whisper in prayer that we need His guidance, but truthfully, we want the headlights to shine on every patch of our path from here all the way to Heaven.

Lately, when I've felt the need to pray for guidance, I've discovered the following two questions to be valuable:

1. Am I striving to follow God's general instructions in all areas of my life?
2. Am I overlooking any words of wisdom spoken into my life recently or in the past?

This prompts me to pray for God's guidance and consider the direction He's already given that I may have forgotten about. Isn't He good?

But First, Simply Ask

When Eliezer reached the well in Abraham's ancestral territory, he followed what he knew to do as far as he could. But then, he faced the unknown. How could he possibly find the next best step in this seemingly impossible task? He had "driven the car with the headlights on" as far as possible, and now it was time for specifics.

His mind likely raced, and his heart may have too. But his experience of watching Abraham serve God and pray at every opportune moment must have come into play because Eliezer then set another example for us. When the general direction needed to develop into something more specific, he did what we often fail to do: He stopped and asked God for directions.

Novel idea, right?

Pausing to pray for specific guidance pivots our attention away from whatever we lack and toward the Lord. I wonder how many of us are directionally challenged because we simply forget to pause and ask God for His guidance. What could serve as a reminder to put on the brakes at critical intersections and pray? I outlined this Prayer Direction Guide: five practical reminders to help us pause, pray, and pivot when precise directions are necessary.

1. Begin the day by asking for God's guidance.
2. Use the initial emotional disturbance as a trigger to pause and pray.
3. Allow God's Word, Spirit, and people to be my daily compass.
4. Embrace number 3 anew whenever I'm starting to stray.
5. Recognize that *feeling* lost doesn't necessarily mean that I am.

Win-Win Prayers

Perhaps when Eliezer arrived at the well with his ten camels, he had that same feeling I'd had as a child when I asked my dad, "How much farther?" Impatience for the next right thing or anxiety over the unknown most likely stirred in his heart and mind. Allowing the emotions to be a signal, he set them aside and did what he knew to do: He prayed. He began by asking the God of Abraham for success for himself and kindness for his master. I suppose some would think this prayer to be self-centered, but it wasn't. Success for himself meant success for his master. It was a win-win prayer!

I believe God is listening for win-win prayers like Eliezer's. Many believers experience guilt when they ask God for success because their upbringing or church background taught them that is selfish or not humble. Somewhere in the back of our minds a voice taunts, *I shouldn't be so needy. I can't ask God to do that. I can't ask God for too much.* But we are prone to misunderstand the heartbeat of our Heavenly Father. What does He want for us as His children? He wants our good and His glory unseparated from one other; this is the epitome of a win-win prayer.

One day, a few months after my Taylor girl had graduated to Heaven, I was reading the Psalms, which had become my daily comfort. The following verse leaped off the page at me: "He will respond to the prayer of the destitute; he will not despise their plea" (Psalm 102:17). I had always thought of a destitute person as someone who is homeless. But upon looking up the word "destitute," I discovered that it means more than that; it is defined as "without means of subsistence; lacking food, clothing, and shelter. deprived of, devoid of, or lacking (often followed by *of*)."[1]

To think *He will respond to the prayer of the lacking* provides a broader understanding than *He will respond to the prayer of the destitute.* Whatever you lack is what God will supply. Do you need success for a business trip, like Eliezer? Your God will supply. He is always listening for your call and won't reject your heart's most resounding cries.

I always pray before I go into the grocery store. One day, I asked God to give me wisdom only to buy what I should and blind me to what I shouldn't. I asked Him to

> *Whatever you lack is what God will supply.*

help me not to worry about what we don't have and focus on His daily provision. "Lord, guide me through the aisles," I said. Then I began my typical shopping pattern, grabbing the cart and checking off the list of necessities as I went.

On that busy Sunday afternoon, when my cart was almost full, an elderly man stopped me.

He held out a stack of papers and said, "Could you use some coupons?"

"I can always use coupons," I said with a grin.

"I hope there's something in there you can use," he replied kindly. And walked away.

I began to look through the stack and discovered a coupon for one item I already had in my cart, but found it was only good if I had two of that item. I returned to the aisle to grab another and met the elderly man once again. He handed me another coupon good for $19 off a purchase of $200 or more at that store and said with a smile, "Now this is one I *know* you can use."

What that man didn't know is that I despise grocery shopping. Inflation is rampant, and feeding a household of seven is no joke. While some might have overlooked the man or thought him strange, I heard God whisper that He's still got the whole world in His hands, especially Aisle Twenty-Four. What a sweet affirmation of God's guidance and direction!

Success and a Sign

Picture Eliezer sitting at the well, a busy town center aflutter with the village women drawing water in preparation for the evening meal. He had made a promise, packed the camels, passed the miles, paused to pray, and petitioned for success. How would he know what to do next? Beyond specific guidance, there would be no way to be totally assured he'd get the outcome he needed.

So he asked God for a sign. (This gets tricky for some modern-day Christians because some of us believe in asking God for signs and some don't.) What audacity Eliezer had! To ask God for success *and* a sign?! Some folks believe that testing God by asking Him for a sign is wrong because how dare we, mortal humans, ask the holy God of the universe for a sign? But Eliezer had to know for sure. He could take no risks in packing up the wrong girl and trekking with her hundreds of miles back to Abraham and Isaac. So he made his request for a specific sign.

> "Lord, God of my master Abraham, make me successful today, and show kindness to my master Abraham. See, I am standing beside this spring, and the daughters of the townspeople are coming out to draw water. May it be that when I say to a young woman, 'Please let down your jar that I may have a drink,' and she says, 'Drink, and I'll water your camels too'—let her be the one you have chosen for your servant Isaac. By this, I will know that you have shown kindness to my master." (Genesis 24:12–14)

If I were a girl at that well, I might have wondered how that man had gotten so far by asking others to help him get a drink. Eliezer was seven hundred miles from home and needed help to get one drink? It probably would have raised some eyebrows. Eliezer knew what he was asking for would be unusual—an extension of hospitality only the most gracious and hard-working girl would offer. Watering all those camels in the heat of the day required not only a generous heart and sturdy back, but also a discerning spirit. The girl had to be able to assess the situation quickly and offer a helping hand.

We have no scriptural explanation for why Eliezer chose this exact sign, but we can understand what he didn't ask for: He didn't ask God to drop the woman from the sky into his lap or have her pop up from the well. His request was not illogical, mystical, or questionable. He used reasoning and wisdom in looking for a sign that would prove her character.

While writing this book, I asked many people if they believed asking God for a sign is good and right. The answers spanned from an emphatic yes to a questionable no and beyond. Eliezer's example is in the Bible, as is God's response—so that leads me to believe we can apply it to our own lives. David's prayer in Psalm 86 supports this principle with verse 17: "Give me a sign of your goodness, that my enemies may see it and be put to shame." This is another win-win prayer example.

Genesis 24:15 begins with a phrase I love: "Before he had finished praying. . . ." Rebekah was already on her way toward Eliezer before he could even finish speaking. God was way ahead of Eliezer! So whether you ask God for a sign or not, know that He is always at work. His timing is not just on time, but perfect.

Mission Possible

In Ohio, summer is a time to enjoy the outdoors as much as possible. One of my prayers during Matt's summer of struggling to find work was that the Lord would provide food, creativity, and entertainment for our family. When we had purchased our house years before, we committed it to the Lord and used it to host small-group Bible studies. As you probably know, hospitality always comes with an element of food and entertainment. I did not know how God would guide us through that season without Matt's income. I simply tried to give everything to Him whenever the thought of "How will I. . . ?" came up.

One Wednesday early that summer, a friend texted to ask if I would like to "shop" her deep freezer for meat for my family. She knew that our budget was tight—well, almost nonexistent—and her invitation couldn't have arrived at a better time. Tears slid down my cheeks as I stocked our own garage freezer with enough meat for dinners and breakfasts for at least three to four weeks.

The next day, I was walking the dog when one of our neighbors asked if we would like to have his grill; he had just purchased a new one and had no use for the old one. I enjoy grilling on the patio in the summer, so of course I said yes. I felt a little silly after he brought it over because Matt and I realized there was no propane tank to go with it. Honestly, every penny mattered, and we didn't think we should spend any money to buy one. But I kept the grill in the corner of the patio and smiled at the Lord's provision.

The following day, Friday, I felt compelled to call one of my old friends, Regina, and ask her to come over for dinner with us. (She is not offended at being called "old" because we've been friends for over twenty years!) The weather was gorgeous, and it seemed the perfect night to enjoy. In the "What's for dinner?" conversation, I mentioned that we could grill some meat—but I didn't have a propane tank. She laughed and replied, "I have one!" In fact, she had a propane tank but no grill! (Seriously, who does this happen to?)

Our neighbor's grill served us that entire summer. My generous, freezer-sharing friend invited me to shop from the overflow of her blessings on four or five other occasions, sustaining us substantially. And Regina shared her propane tank all summer long.

God had gone before our family, just as He did for Eliezer.

He'll do the same for you. His heart is for you; His guidance is available to you. No matter how desperate your request is for Him to lead, He's always ready to do it. He goes before you to prepare the way, even before you pray.

When you ask Him, "Are we there yet?" for the thousandth time, He replies, "We're closer than we've ever been, My child. Closer than we've ever been."

God, Guide Me

God, guide me. Where my soul lacks movement, propel me forward. Prompt my heart to pause and ask for directions. When I can't see as far ahead as I'd like, help me remember that walking the path with You illuminates each step when I need to take it.

Chapter Seven Prayer Principles

- Like a compass, God uses His Word, His Spirit, and His people in tandem to guide us.
- Pausing to pray for specific guidance pivots your attention away from what you lack and toward the Lord.

- God wants our good and His glory unseparated from each other; this is the epitome of a win-win prayer.
- He goes before you to prepare the way, even before you pray.

CHAPTER EIGHT

The Battle Is the Lord's

God, Deliver Me.

Since Taylor's terminal diagnosis at age four, I knew the day would come when her battle with the disease would end. However, not knowing when it would end was difficult, and my desperation for her to be well escalated as her suffering worsened in the last weeks of her life.

I've never felt as helpless as I did when she gasped for breath, hour after hour. I must have whispered a thousand times for her to go to Jesus. I told her that Mommy couldn't fix it and make it all better. I reminded her that she needed a new body, and that Heaven would give her one. I begged God to come and scoop her up, praying, "Lord, have mercy. Deliver her."

But Taylor was a fighter. She came into this world fighting for each breath. She lived each day fighting to do things I often take for granted. Taylor would leave no other way than still fighting. I mentioned earlier that I will never forget the day she proudly announced, at her Sunday School teacher's request, "The battle is the Lord's." There had never been a time where I needed this truth to be more palpable than in the days of her final fight.

As I would learn in the days following Taylor's heavenly homegoing, deliverance would be a daily necessity.

It Wasn't One and Done

During the 2023 PGA Championship, the crowd cheered on Michael Block, a humble, forty-six-year-old who had never before qualified for a major championship, all week long. After qualifying for the major tournament through exceptional circumstances and making the cut as others struggled, he headed into the final round as a fan favorite. It didn't seem like his game could improve—nor did it need to—until he arrived at Hole Thirteen. Aiming carefully at the green, Block hit the ball like a beeline to the pin, where it sank into the cup in a dramatic hole-in-one, and the crowd went wild.[1] You've got to love a good underdog story.

Underdog competitions are often called "David and Goliath" matchups even today. We admire David's courage to run toward the giant Philistine in battle, and our hearts swell with pride in him when he slung the stone into Goliath's uncovered forehead, winning a battle on behalf of his nation and shutting down the fear that had prevailed over the people for so long. Such an enormous victory is one to be cherished and fosters our love for long-shot heroes.

But I have wrestled with the fact that as great as this victory was, it was only one of the first battles of a long war. Yes, David had sharpened his skills on the lion and the bear; now, he had taken down Goliath. But 1 Samuel continues to tell us about all the battles David fought before finally sitting on the throne of Israel twenty-seven years later.[2] Yes, twenty-seven years! How do we wrap our minds around the fact that his battle with Goliath was far from a one-and-done deal for him?

David wrote many of his psalms during those twenty-seven years, so those years of waiting clearly weren't wasted. I've always appreciated the background story of a written work, and the Davidic Psalms escort us on a journey through fields and caves. The superscription of Psalm 56 notes, "Of David, When the Philistines had seized him in Gath." Psalm 57 explains David wrote it "when he had fled from Saul into the cave." Psalms 57–59 were all written by David to the tune of a song called "Do Not Destroy." Psalm 59's superscription shares that David wrote it when Saul sent men to surveil his house and kill him. It's as if David's creative songwriting juices only began to flow when he was held practically at sword point. But when we examine these chapters, we find that sometimes parts of those psalms, or even all of them, are not only songs, but prayers David sang to God in his distress. "Be merciful to me . . . have mercy on me . . . I cry out . . . deliver me from my enemies, O God."

While his physical enemies loomed large, David understood from the beginning of his face-off with Goliath that the battle itself was even more significant than it seemed. David didn't have just one enemy, but many. Even those in his own camp sometimes turned against him (Psalm 55). Though Goliath was physically larger than everyone else, David recognized the real enemy wasn't Goliath, but the devil; he also never forgot that as fiercely as he might attack David's country, heart, and mind, God still reigned over him.

Because the spiritual warfare raging against him was strong, David always took prayer seriously. We tend to think of crying out to God as a pitiful response to our need for help; however, David shows us that crying out to God to move us out of situations isn't disgraceful, but a shameless plug for the deliverance God already knows we need. Desperate prayer is a wise admission, not a weak acceptance.

> *Desperate prayer is a wise admission, not a weak acceptance.*

The Actual Whole Armor of God

Today, we often think of a person, a situation, or a set of circumstances as our enemy. Sometimes, it can feel like society or money wage war on our hearts. Disease can certainly feel like a human foe. But all of those things are tools Satan uses against us. He is the real enemy. As God's child, Satan hates you and does everything he can to twist your thoughts into a cyclone of confusion, negativity, and despair.

I can still see the three-by-five-foot poster of a soldier in full gear hanging on the wall of my Sunday School classroom— the image that officially taught me about the armor of God. "Be strong in God's mighty power" was written in bold print across the top. This part appealed to me as a kid, but who or what were we fighting against? Quite some time would pass before I could begin to understand:

> For we do not wrestle against flesh and blood, but against the rulers, against the authorities, against the cosmic powers over this present darkness, against the spiritual forces of evil in the heavenly places. (Ephesians 6:12)

Dear Christian, in case you haven't noticed, we are in a war for our souls, our lives, and ultimately, God's glory. Satan will do anything to prevent us from asking Jesus to save our souls, live our lives for Christ, and bring glory to God. Period. End of story. Peter said it this way:

> Be alert and of sober mind. Your enemy, the devil, prowls around like a roaring lion, looking for someone to devour. Resist him, standing firm in the faith, because you know that the family of believers worldwide suffers the same suffering. (1 Peter 5:7–9)

That giant poster mentioned above listed each piece of armor needed to fight the enemy: the belt of truth, the breastplate of righteousness, feet prepared with the gospel of peace, the shield of faith, the helmet of salvation, and the sword of the Spirit, which is God's Word. It's easy to get so focused on the physical pieces of armor symbolizing spiritual war tools that we lump Ephesians 6:10–17 together and call it a day, because the passage ends with "Take the helmet of salvation and the sword of the Spirit, which is the word of God." Armor complete, Sir. *Salute.*

But notice the next verse, Ephesians 6:18:

> *And* pray in the Spirit on all occasions with all kinds of prayers and requests. With this in mind, be alert and always keep on praying for all the Lord's people. (emphasis mine)

See that "and"? You can't put the armor of God on by itself and expect to succeed against evil. So why did Paul include prayer as part of the armor of God?

Because no battle can be won without communication with one's Commanding Officer.

> *No battle can be won without communication with one's Commanding Officer.*

Defining Spiritual Warfare and Spiritual Attacks

I've heard people say, "I'm not one to label every little setback as 'spiritual warfare,'" and I understand that view. But what is spiritual warfare, and what is a spiritual attack? The word "warfare" is a generalized term that I would define as "struggle." Dictionary.com uses the word "conflict." Every Christian on the planet is engaged in some level of spiritual warfare; Peter warned us of that, as we read above. We all struggle with various temptations. Author Jim Maxim explains it this way:

> Satan can never possess a Christian; our spirits have been born again in Christ. However, he can oppress or influence us with relentless thoughts of depression, anxiety, fear, unbelief, lust, anger, unforgiveness, insecurity, and addictions that create strongholds in our lives.[3]

Every day, we encounter issues designed to pull us away from God. But the devil is targeted and specific. He looks for weaknesses in our armor. He is ever tempting and trying, but he is lazy. He uses the same tactics over and over again because they work. When he sees God's glory on the horizon, and he sees you are about to experience a victory or influence someone for good, you'd better look out; this is prime time for a spiritual attack, a more specifically targeted area of trial or temptation. Paul called it "the day of evil." In other words, the enemy knows what our hot buttons are and the best time to use them against us.

It may sound trivial to some, but one of my triggers is car problems. You could chalk this up to the fact that I am about as mechanically inclined as a mouse, but for whatever reason, encountering vehicle issues gets under my skin big-time. Remember that story I told you about the flat tire earlier?

You'll never believe what happened a few days after I finished writing that chapter.

I went to my 2008 Honda Odyssey, which has been as reliable as the miraculous oil in the widow's jars for over a decade, to find it had a flat tire. Only this time, the screw that had punctured it was close to the outer edge, and it couldn't be repaired; I had to buy a new tire. Then, just a few weeks ago, one of my teenagers ran over *another* screw that flattened the new tire. This time, it was inconvenient, but it could be plugged.

Why the "sudden" onslaught of tire issues? Because the enemy knows how car problems escalate in my mind. He also knows the battle it takes for me to put words to the page in this busy season with my family. He attacks methodically and escalates as he sees the need. He tries to distract me from the work God has called me to do. This usually comes in the form of busyness and takes virtually no effort on his part. This level of aggression is subtle and simple for him. The old saying goes, "If the devil can't make you bad, he'll make you busy."

If that doesn't work, he will try to discourage me. (Hence, the second flat tire. The first one didn't send me down the path he had hoped for.) As silly as it may sound, flat tires send me into a frenzy of thoughts like: *I'm not equipped to do this. I don't enjoy doing this. Why does this always happen to me?* I can change a flat, but I don't enjoy it. I can pay for a new tire, but I certainly don't enjoy that, either. I think: *How will we pay for this? We already have enough bills to pay.* Transitioning my thoughts from a simple flat tire to a large-family, financially complex budget issue can easily discourage me.

Then, if the devil's tricks of distraction and discouragement don't work, he'll try a detour. The trip to the tire store steals the block of time that I had set aside to work for the day. Then I'm bombarded with thoughts like, *I'm falling behind on this project, and I'm never going to be able to accomplish it in a timely fashion. In fact, I have struggled to earn a living from writing; why am I even doing this?* The enemy hopes I'll stay in this place long enough to destroy what God has intended for my good and His glory.

On Satan's best days of work, detours lead to derailment. In my case, you can see that he hasn't won yet—after all, I'm still writing! But we've all witnessed the many heartbreaking periods when distraction became discouragement. The discouragement then led to a detour, eventually derailing a testimony. And it took us a while to get back on track.

Tires might not be your spiritual pain point, but the enemy always uses this same old formula. He wants to distract, discourage, detour, and derail you.

> *On Satan's best days of work, detours lead to derailment.*

What does desperate prayer have to do with that? I'm so glad you asked.

Prayer as a Weapon

If you ever need good reading material to help you fall asleep, open the book of 1 Chronicles. (OK, I'm kidding. Slightly.) The first heading above Chapter 1 reads "historical records from

Adam to Abraham." Genealogy is important to God; this long history of "the sons of, the father of, and so-and-so begat so-and-so" causes me to sit up and take notice of the rude interruption in Chapter 5.

> The Reubenites, the Gadites and the half-tribe of Manasseh had 44,760 men ready for military service—able-bodied men who could handle shield and sword, who could use a bow, and who were trained for battle. They waged war against the Hagrites, Jetur, Naphish and Nodab. They were helped in fighting them, and God delivered the Hagrites and all their allies into their hands, because they cried out to him during the battle. He answered their prayers, because they trusted in him. (1 Chronicles 5:18–20)

These strong warriors had the necessary weapons and the experience to use them. But even though they were battle-ready, they still needed God to do what they could not do for themselves, so they cried out to Him. Their humble calls revealed their total reliance on Him. God longs for hearts that wholly lean on His power and strength. His strength is made perfect in our weakness. The summary of the above story is found in 1 Chronicles 5:22: "because the battle was God's." The Israelites had discovered the same truth David knew before fighting Goliath.

If you are in the thick of a battle today and don't know how to keep going, understand that God knows you need deliverance. I don't know if your battle is cancer or heart disease, money or marital issues, sickness or sadness, but I know that God longs to be your first call for help in the battle. While the deliverance you long for may not look like what you think it should, God is with you. Humbly seek Him. Lay your heart bare before Him. Let Him know you need His strength and power and rely on His daily deliverance. Until the day God calls us home, we'll be waging war against the enemy, but we are still assured of victory. Billy Graham once declared, "I've read the last page of the Bible; it's all going to turn out all right."[4]

Our oldest daughter used to tell Matt, "I wanna do it all by imselves, Daddy." Isn't that us, too? We want to do it by ourselves. And when we can't, when we're in over our heads, that's

> *God longs to be your first call for help in the battle.*

often when we humble ourselves before the Lord and say, "God, it's bigger than me. I need You, Lord. I need You to rescue me."

I am proof that God delivers by His power. One of the most brutal truths I've had to claim over my heart is that I did not die when my daughter died. This means God has a purpose for my life and will continue to deliver me daily until I go to Heaven. And I know He will do that for you, too. In God's purpose, you can find your way; make His daily guidance where you long to stay. The battle truly is the Lord's.

Oh, and guess what? This morning when I went to the van to take one of my daughters to school, the tire hazard light was on in the dashboard.

God, Deliver Me

God, deliver me. Though the enemy chases my soul, remind me through Your Spirit that You are my refuge and fortress. I can run to You and be safe. No matter the occasion, let prayer be my wise weapon of choice.

Chapter Eight Prayer Principles

- Prayer is a shameless plug for the help God already knows we need.
- Desperate prayer is a wise admission, not a weak acceptance.
- No battle can be won without communication with one's Commanding Officer.
- On Satan's best days of work, detours lead to derailment.
- In God's purpose, you can find your way; make His daily guidance where you long to stay.

CHAPTER NINE

Speechless

God, Fill Me.

The note began: *I know you are a praying woman.* The woman who wrote this note had also lost her daughter, though her circumstances were completely different than mine. I felt honored to receive her prayer request, but my heart sank as I read the desperate details of her story. I whispered, "Jesus, have mercy. I don't know how to pray for this new friend. I can't wrap my head around her situation."

Compassionate grief washed over me, triggering a fresh flood of personal sorrow. I wept and wished the world wasn't filled with suffering and despair. I dried the tears with the backs of my hands, and a sigh escaped. Then a groan.

Perhaps you've experienced that same kind of groan. The feeling lies deep within your soul and sometimes slips out without warning. Or maybe it steeped for a whole day before exploding like a strong espresso's bitter flavor. Groans are the inarticulate sounds of pain.

Exodus 2 shows us the children of Israel as enslaved people groaning in Egypt. For 430 years, they had lived in a foreign land, serving their Egyptian taskmasters in hard labor. The painful work had grown so intense that they cried out in their forlorn state. God heard their cries and remembered His promise to Abraham, Isaac, and Jacob. I'm not sure from Scripture if their cries had words attached, but we know God took note: "So God looked on the Israelites and was concerned about them" (Exodus 2:25).

Exodus 3 begins, "Now Moses. . . ." The contrast of this moment is marked clearly: God had been preparing a man to answer the Israelites' prayers. While they may not have been able to string more than a few words together in prayer, He had already positioned a burning bush in front of Moses to jumpstart the process of answering.

Here's where I find this situation a little comical: The children of Israel used unintelligible sounds to get God's attention, and His response was to send Moses, a former murderer with a speech impediment. Everyone involved is inarticulate, yet

God is not bothered by human limitations. The drought is where His glory shines the greatest.

When Moses told God his speech impediment was an obstacle to confronting Pharaoh, God said,

> "Who gave human beings their mouths? Who makes them deaf or mute? Who gives them sight or makes them blind? Is it not I, the Lord? Now go; I will help you speak and will teach you what to say." (Exodus 4:11)

Just as He supplied the power, God would also supply the necessary words.

Over the years of hosting small groups in our home, I've heard many people from all walks of life shy away from prayer, occasionally even admitting, "I don't know how to pray." Sometimes, that means they don't know how to talk to God because they can't see Him. Other times, it means they aren't sure how to communicate because there are different types of conversation, such as thanksgiving, confession, praise, or requests. But then there are times when life is so challenging and twisted that the words simply refuse to escape our lips. They stall before reaching our tongues and float around in our minds without forming complete thoughts. Our

> *Just as He supplied the power, God would also supply the necessary words.*

emotions and intellect fail to unite except in the agony of a loss
for words, and the silence is deafening.

When You Don't Know What to Pray

I don't have the date scribbled in my prayer journal, but some
years after Taylor's diagnosis, Matt and I stopped praying for
her healing to happen on this side of Heaven. I suppose some
would think this was a lack of faith, and some people actually
did accuse us of being faithless. But the truth was that, while
I felt full of confidence, I sometimes didn't know what to pray.
It seemed to me that God had created Taylor uniquely, and
His plan for her life existed as one of a kind. My knowledge
of her disease was limited by science itself, and as intuitive as
I was about her needs, I had a limited understanding of her
body's convoluted processes. Medical professionals often
struggled to define her symptoms and piece the problem areas
together, especially since Taylor could not describe her pain
to us. So I often found myself trying to pray and coming up
empty, without a single cohesive thought.

The Apostle Paul knew the sound of agony well. In his letter to the Roman church, he told them God could hear the cries
of the earth: "We know that the whole creation has been
groaning as in the pains of childbirth right up to the present
time" (Romans 8:22). He further explained that the physical
and emotional pain we experience in this world will not stop
until our bodies are redeemed in Heaven. There we will share
the restoration and redemption of Jesus fully, but until then,

there will be moans and groans over things we cannot comprehend. Life is hard. (Like I need to tell you that.)

But Paul doesn't leave us in despair, and neither does our loving Savior. When grief and sorrow gripped my heart, the Lord brought Paul's writings to me beautifully, and I clung to the words he penned all those years ago: "In the same way, the Spirit helps us in our weakness" (Romans 8:26).

Weak, indeed. As I watched Sweet T's daily suffering, my weakness deepened. There is no weakness like that of total dependence on someone else. And yet, in that very weakness, when we become totally dependent on God because all earthly control has been stripped away, He provides the Spirit as our Intercessor. Thank you, Lord, for not leaving us speechless and alone.

I honestly didn't know how to pray for my sweet Taylor girl. Did I ask God to heal her when her very DNA contained the code for her disease? Yes, and many people might say that was the only correct thing to pray for—you should never stop praying for a miracle. But what if God had actually designed the benefit I wanted to see on this planet to be revealed only in Heaven? I began to believe that His plan was bigger than I could comprehend, but the burden was too heavy for my frail shoulders. The monumental situation, with all its details, stole my ability to know what to ask for. Romans 8:26 says, "We do not know what we ought to pray for . . ." This was me. How do you pray while someone you love is dying?

But the end of that verse became my prayer mantra: ". . . the Spirit himself intercedes for us through wordless groans." I didn't have to have words to pray; I could bow before the Lord in spirit, yielding to Him in my weakness. I could give myself to what the Spirit would say for me. And although sometimes groans escaped my lips and at other times, I fell silent before Him, the Spirit of God interceded with Father God on my behalf. He knew what Taylor needed. He knew what I needed. And He knows what you need today.

How does He know what we need? The Holy Spirit lives inside us, so He intimately knows our thoughts, even when we cannot form them into words.

Think about the power of God's words for a minute. "Let there be light" were the words He used to begin creation. Genesis 1:2 explains that the earth was formless and empty; darkness lay over the surface of the deep, and the Spirit of God was hovering over the waters. The Creator of the universe sculpted the entire world into existence, starting from scratch, through only His voice. And while it seems miraculous enough that He should use words to create the earth, what I know to be true from my own life is that when I am formless and empty, without words, God's Spirit is hovering over my heart. His communication with Father God is so clear, so concise, that it is unintelligible to my human ears. I love the way Romans 8:26 uses the phrase "wordless groans." When God the Spirit speaks with God the Father, words are unnecessary for communication. They do not need to converse as you and I do when we talk with one another. Their love language is not one we can wrap our heads around. It's too powerful, intimate, and infinite for human comprehension.

While watching my daughter suffer and die, I discovered that when nothing is left of me, when I am speechless, I am in a great place. God showed up and showed off when the world was dark and formless. This proves I can take heart in my Creator's supernatural abilities.

Got nothing? In a dark place? You're in a fabulous space for God to do incredible things. His seemingly impossible work often begins in a dark place with absolutely nothing. When your needs are too deep for words, embrace the Holy Spirit, Whose wordless whisper speaks volumes on your behalf. You may not understand how this prayer for you works, but that's faith. Faith believes in the unseen. Prayer is an exercise in trust.

If you've ever started a new workout regimen, you know it isn't comfortable. Real change requires persistent effort. So don't give up on praying to God when you are left without words. Let the Holy Spirit living in you communicate on your behalf. Yield your heart to His skill. A little "let" can go a long way. If "let there be light" resulted in galaxies even the most powerful tools have yet to discover, imagine what might be possible when you yield to the Spirit of God and the words He speaks on your behalf.

> *If "let there be light" resulted in galaxies even the most powerful tools have yet to discover, imagine what might be possible when you yield to the Spirit of God and the words He speaks on your behalf.*

Showing Up without Words

Sparkling cornfields danced alongside the road; the farther north I drove, the more fallen snow shimmered across the plains. A lone hearse sat in the church parking lot where I pulled in. When I stepped out of the van, the coldness of the air declared the season's rigidity. Kent was a young man who had been battling the same disease Taylor had, and he had just lost his final battle. I was there to grieve with his family.

The time between entering the church and leaving the graveside felt sacred and holy. Respect and awe for all God had done through this single life filled the church. One can't ask for much more on this earth than to experience a well-loved life. The truth is, we are all well loved by our Creator; we just don't always realize it.

So grief sat amid grace.

Upon seeing Kent's mama and sisters, whom I've known for many years, tears slipped out and rolled down my cheeks. I hadn't planned on crying—but I hadn't planned on not crying, either. I had no agenda other than to let Kent's family know my heart ached for them. I simply showed up.

I stood by his casket, and jumbled thoughts flooded my mind. A wonderful slideshow played on the overhead screen while Kent's family and I spoke for a bit. I began to understand what his last weeks of life had been like as he battled the same disease my Taylor girl was still fighting at that time. I grieved for Kent's physical pain and suffering. I suffered for his parents in their watches by night. I grieved for his sisters in their loss, and I grieved because I wanted my precious daughter to be spared from all those things. The combination of angst for Taylor and grief for Kent's family left me confused and disoriented.

One of Kent's teenaged sisters was sitting in the row behind me. I felt the Holy Spirit leading me to sit beside her, so I did and placed my arm around her. Her body shook with sobs. She put her hand on my lap and her head on my shoulder, and we mourned—really mourned.

I didn't trust myself to try to speak. Truthfully, the words were stuck like a wrecked train off the track. All I could do was say in my spirit, "Jesus, comfort Your daughter." I want to tell you that I was brave and bold and just sat there and hugged her while she received strength from me, but I'm not humanly capable of that. It was all too overwhelming. Yet somehow, physically holding her in her grief ushered in an enormous sense of peace from the Lord. I could think only, "Rejoice with those who rejoice and weep with those who weep."

I had received the hallowed opportunity to weep with a friend. Not from a distance, not standing beside her, but letting waves of anguish wash over us without restraint, grieving together that we might comfort one another with the comfort by which we are comforted. In the beauty of giving one another permission to ache freely, we also experienced the Holy Spirit as Comforter. It was a moment I will never forget.

Yet no words were uttered or exchanged in those minutes. I simply showed up, and the Spirit Who hovers around God's throne ministered to us. I'm so grateful.

Open Your Mouth

So far in this chapter, I have shared only about voids. The first empty space was where the Israelites found themselves in slavery, most likely unable to frame sentences to express their need for God to intervene. That led us to Moses's stuttering mouth, which gave him such a feeling of inadequacy that he told God to find someone else to lead the Israelites to freedom.

Each of these situations shows a lack of words. It would seem that the answer to having no words to pray is allowing the Holy Spirit to intercede on our behalf. While that's a portion of the cure, it's not all of it. As glorious as it is to have the Holy Spirit as our intercessor, there's more. So much more.

Psalm 81:7 describes how God used Moses to deliver the Israelites from slavery: "In your distress you called and I rescued you."

Nonetheless, they continued to experience bondage to their desires—they wanted meat when He had already provided manna. God said to them, "I am the Lord your God, who brought you up out of Egypt. Open your mouth wide, and I will fill it" (Psalm 81:10). Can you see what He wanted to do for them? That state of emptiness and longing didn't have to be permanent. They attempted to fill their voids with stuff, their wants, and even other gods. But God implored, "Let me fulfill you."

God not only wants to be your Rescue, but your Refill. He wants to do more than take you out of Egypt; He wants to do more than walk you through the desert. He wants to intercede and supply all your needs because *He* is all you need. He longs for you to see that His provision and power are abundant and fulfilling. Pure contentment is found when we rely on His Spirit to fill us up to overflowing because we have allowed our speechlessness to send us to our knees. But while on our knees, we must embrace our barren shells and refuse to refill them with anything less than what our Creator wants for us.

After my Taylor girl exchanged her jacked-up earthly body for her heavenly one, I feared I would forget how much I needed the Lord. Taylor's needs had kept me tethered to Jesus. I thought that per-

> *God not only wants to be your Rescue, but your Refill.*

haps I would grow accustomed to living in a new state that didn't include a lack of speech, seizures, or middle-of-the-night wakeups. Our family had lived an abnormal life for so long that something about a typical family life without constant urgent medical needs seemed too easy. Would I continue to rely on my God and call out to Him for every need, regardless of its seeming lack of intensity? Would I recognize that I required His oxygen for *every* breath, not just gasps?

I soon found that the decades of running to Him in prayer when I was speechless were the training ground for the marathon of not only Taylor's life, but my own. The moments spent on my knees without speech to voice my needs taught me to allow the Holy Spirit to interact with God the Father for my benefit. In the silence, I have learned to open my mouth wide and ask God to fill it to overflowing.

It's a hard-won prayer we each must embrace daily as our own: God, fill me.

God, Fill Me

God, my mind is in shambles, and the words won't come. Nothing in life feels cohesive, and I'm a hot mess, Lord. I don't even know what to pray. Thank You for Your Spirit, Who prays on my behalf. Let me not forget that He lives in me. I am nothing and have nothing. God, fill me.

Chapter Nine Prayer Principles

- God is not bothered in the least by human limitations; our lack is where His glory shines the brightest.
- The Holy Spirit's wordless whispers speak volumes on your behalf.
- God's seemingly impossible work often begins in a dark place with absolutely nothing.
- God not only wants to be your Rescue, but your Refill.

CHAPTER TEN

No Way Out

God, Show Me.

As far back as I can remember, I have struggled with eye infections. If you saw my high school senior photos, my red eyes would make you want to take a tissue to the image.

Despite many trips to various doctors, my parents could not find the right resources to help me. Weepy, bloodshot eyes were my norm as a child, no matter what we tried.

Finally, after my freshman year of college, a trip to see my uncle, who was an optometrist, revealed that I had ulcers eating through the corneas of both eyes, particularly the left. No wonder I really struggled to see! Especially in the dark—I typically had to feel my way around when the lights were dim. My uncle said if I didn't get a cornea transplant immediately, I'd lose my left eye entirely.

After sitting in the hospital for four days waiting for a cornea to become available, I finally had the surgery on my left eye; I would have to wait a year for the second transplant. Though the vision in my left eye remained somewhat blurry even after the surgery, my right eye improved quickly with treatment, and I relied on it heavily.

A year later, the second transplant was performed. A few days afterward, we removed the bandage over my eye to test my vision, and I noticed a change once my eyes adjusted to light again. Things seemed a little clearer than they had been for years, but I still had a long way to go in the healing process.

The hospital where I'd had my surgery was in Atlanta; after a few days, my parents and I began the long drive home to West Virginia. As the hours passed, I noticed I could see the road signs before we got to them. I could hardly contain my excitement and began to talk about all the things I could see as if I were seeing for the first time. Details and distance were no longer a challenge, and the world had come alive for me in a brand-new way.

My parents sat in the front seat, unable to speak. I can still see them in my mind's eye. Through tears, their eyes locked briefly in sweet victory. Every sacrifice they'd made had been worth it. God had answered their prayers and saved their girl's vision.

I remind myself of this story often so that I won't forget the blessing of sight I was given. If you are a blind person listening to this book, my heart aches for you. I look forward to the day when your heavenly eyesight outshines my current earthly vision. How we will see with our eyes in Heaven is beyond my imagination.

But until then, how can we pray to see the spiritual forest around us, not just the trees?

The Need to Escape

In 2 Kings 6:8–23, we find Elisha, the prophet of God, serving as a spy for the king of Israel during a war with the Arameans. The Lord would tell Elisha details about where the enemy was camping and planned to attack, and Elisha passed those on to the king. The Aramean king thought someone in the army was a traitor because no matter his strategy, Israel eluded him. Upon grilling his officers, he discovered the prophet of God was to blame, and immediately decided to put an end to him. When word came that Elisha was staying in Dothan, the king of Aram sent a "strong force" to surround the city by night (2 Kings 6:13). Nothing like a surprise attack to take the prophet down a notch, right?

The next morning when Elisha's servant (I'll call him "Buck," since we don't know his name) left the house, all he could see were horses and chariots surrounding it for miles, and he shook in his boots. (Alright, sandals.) "Oh no!" he said to Elisha. "What are we going to do?"

But Elisha was cool, calm, and collected. Unalarmed. Unafraid. Elisha answered, "Don't be afraid. Those who are with us are more than those who are with them."

I can see Buck rolling his eyes and thinking Elisha needed to have his eyes checked. But at that moment, Elisha prayed— and not for a way out of the situation, like, "Lord, get us out of here . . . Father, rescue us from the enemy . . . Jesus, open a back door, for heaven's sake!" (No, none of those words were chosen, though I'm game for any of those pleas!)

> Elisha prayed, "Open his eyes, Lord, so that he may see."
> Then the Lord opened the servant's eyes, and he looked and saw the hills full of horses and chariots of fire all around Elisha. (2 Kings 6:17)

Talk about eye-opening! I wonder just how far Buck's jaw dropped. He thought he and Elisha were both goners—until his spiritual sight was activated. He had been blinded to the reality that the mighty army of God was there to fight on his behalf. But once the man of God prayed on his behalf, he could see just how great his God's defense was.

Looking up in prayer is always better than looking for a way out of a situation.

Looking up in prayer is always better than looking for a way out of a situation.

Foresight over Hindsight

You've heard the saying "Hindsight is 20/20." Many of us have worked to improve our spiritual hindsight and gotten it as close to 20/20 as possible. We want to see the hand of God in our past situations, hoping to see the good that's come out of them. When hard circumstances bounce into our lives, we strive to learn God's lessons for us in them. We take Scripture to heart and exclaim, "Lord, I won't do that again." Then the Spirit of God helps us remember His promises and our commitment to Him, empowering us to follow through.

But like Buck, when we find ourselves in a full-on spiritual attack, all we can see is how big the enemy is and that he surrounds us. It seems there is no way to escape, and we forget that "the one who is in you is greater than the one who is in the world" (1 John 4:4).

I've found that when the panoramic view of life seems full of nothing but doom, gloom, and despair, prayer is the most pivotal choice I can make.

If, by some chance, you're thinking, "Rachel, you already wrote a chapter about asking for God's guidance. Isn't this the same thing?" then I must say that praying for God to guide is asking Him for direction, while praying for God to show up is asking Him for revelation. To show is to reveal, and to guide is to lead. Asking

> *Praying for God to guide is asking Him for direction, while praying for God to show up is asking Him for revelation.*

God to show me how He is working comes before we start down the path. This prayer includes showing me my purpose, my mission, or what I am missing.

Learning from our past mistakes is noble, but how much further would we get if we added spiritual foresight to our tool belt?

Paul said it this way to the church in Ephesus:

> I pray that the eyes of your heart may be enlightened so that you may know the hope to which he has called you, the riches of his glorious inheritance in his holy people and his incomparably great power for us who believe that power is the same as the mighty strength he exerted when he raised Christ from the dead and seated him at his right hand in the heavenly realms, far above all rule and authority, power and dominion, and every name that is invoked, not only in the present age but also in the one to come. . . .
> (Ephesians 1:18–21)

I've discovered that praying, "God, show me," usually begins with a nudge from the Holy Spirit. And if I'm not aware, without the eyes of my heart peeled wide open to recognize the hope to which God is calling me, then I won't experience His riches or His power in a situation.

Cake in Point

On a typical Monday morning, I opened Facebook to post for the day. My notifications led me to a local community group, where a woman I didn't know had posted a request: She needed a pumpkin cake with cream cheese frosting before 8 p.m. It seemed like a long shot, but she was asking if anyone could bake it for her.

I felt immediately drawn to do it. I can't explain why, except that I have learned to listen when the Holy Spirit gives me that heart nudge. Baking is my therapy. So I messaged her.

When she came by to pick it up, she explained, "It's my dad's birthday." It was sweet of her to be so specific about his favorite kind of cake.

That woman had no idea that my own father's first birthday in heaven would be two days later. After she left, God whispered to my heart, *I knew you'd enjoy making a cake to celebrate your dad's birthday even though he's with Me.*

Isn't God amazing? I thought I was blessing that woman, and while the Lord did use me to do that, He had a beautiful blessing for me tied up in that situation all along.

What if I had responded to the Holy Spirit's prompts by saying, "Oh, it's Monday morning, and I can't add anything else on my plate today." Truthfully, it was an unusually busy week with Tuesday through Thursday packed full—but Monday and Friday were both free of appointments.

What if I had said, "It's weird to bake a cake for a stranger"? I agree that's not exactly the norm. Still, I've always been attracted to Hebrews 13:2, which says, "Do not forget to show hospitality to strangers, for by so doing some people have shown hospitality to angels without knowing it." I also knew I already had all the ingredients for that cake. That alone is a miracle at my house!

What's most interesting is that in my personal prayer time with the Lord, before I ever went to Facebook, I had prayed, "Father, show me the work You have for me today. Broaden my perspective to see more than what is right in front of me. Move me to interact with people in a way that reflects who You are." God is so good that my willingness to step out in faith on someone else's behalf resulted in a sweet gift from Him to my heart.

Remember Paul's words in Ephesians 1:18–21? "I pray that the eyes of your heart may be enlightened so that you may know the hope to which he has called you." Paul knew that the Christians in Ephesus needed spiritual foresight to see beyond what was right in front of them. They lacked awareness of what was available to them as God's children. He also knew that prayer would be the key to removing the blinders.

The Spiritual Prayer Forest

Earlier, I asked how we can pray to see the spiritual forest, not just the trees. The spiritual forest is God's plan, purpose, and perspective for all humanity; the trees are individual aspects of our personal lives or opportunities to serve Him. God is growing this mighty spiritual forest of His overarching eternal plan, and He uses our daily lives and tasks as part of that plan. Sometimes we plant seeds, and sometimes we water those others have already planted.

Our part of God's spiritual forest might look like being a greeter at church or baking a cake for a stranger. It's easy to hyper-focus on the "proper" place to serve. I've been guilty of overthinking God's will to the point of forgetting that my first step is always just raw surrender and willingness. I've often been so caught up in my to-do list that I lost sight of the spiritual forest for the trees. The "God, show me" prayer becomes critical in this scenario.

I wasn't looking for a Facebook post when I prayed to God the morning I made that cake. And I certainly wasn't thinking about cake. Rather, my desperate heart craved my Heavenly Father because my earthly father was no longer here to hold me. Surrender to desperation drew me to cry out for God to show me Himself in those circumstances. When we show up, God often shows off.

I've heard people say they've asked God to show them what to do, and nothing happened. They desperately needed a way out of a situation, like Elisha's servant.

> *When we show up, God often shows off.*

They were looking for an escape, but there was none to be found. The problem wasn't that God wasn't showing them the way; it was that they were looking for Him in the wrong places. Their eyes were open but focused on their own ideas. They were scanning for potential in areas that felt obvious or familiar.

Maybe the tree of opportunity you're searching for looks nothing like you think it will. What can we expect to see when asking, "God, show me?"

I See Men as Trees Walking

The stories of Jesus healing people in the New Testament have always drawn my attention, but a particular blind man's story told in Mark 8:22–25 pulls me in even deeper. We have no idea what caused his blindness, but we know he had friends. Those friends saw hope on the horizon and took him to Jesus.

Jesus held the blind man by the hand and led him outside town. Say what you will, but for me, this is a reminder that some folks won't be reached in the public square. We've got to have relationships that go beyond the church walls. (Sorry, little sidebar there.)

Think about how that man must have been feeling. For at least most of his life, if not all of it, he'd been led around by the hand. I'm guessing he had learned not to take just any hand, but only the hands of those who had proven trustworthy. But on that day, he let a man he'd never met lead him outside the protection of the village. This required a certain amount of faith.

What happened next would challenge anyone's faith: the man then allowed Jesus to spit on his eyes. Who had ever heard of using saliva for healing? But when he opened his eyes, the man could see! Miraculously and gloriously, Jesus had restored his sight! Talk about an eye-opening experience. There was only one problem.

Jesus asked him, "Do you see anything?"

He replied, "I see men as trees walking."

Enter a new level of faith: He had to tell Jesus the truth. He could have said, "I'm good." He could have answered, "Yes, I can see." I wonder how the story would have played out if he had been content with the ability to see things but not clearly. Would he have lived with a distorted vision for the rest of his life because he settled for "good enough"? But instead, he honestly told the Lord, "I can see, but it's a confusing world. I need more of what You gave me, Jesus. Perfect my sight."

Some of us pray, "God, show me," but we still need a clear vision because we are in the perfecting process—what is known as sanctification. The Lord longs to improve our spiritual eyesight, but He also wants us to learn to rely on Him entirely. We might miss the spiritual forest for the trees if we accept the fact that we can see, but not perfectly. However, when we whisper, "God, I see what You might be showing me, but I'm only human and need more. Give me another touch, will You?" His hand of healing brings crystal-clear vision.

God sees everything that we cannot. Prayer reveals possibilities we didn't know existed, exposes provision we couldn't have predicted, and demonstrates the power we wouldn't otherwise experience. Begging "God, show me" holds the potential for a show-stopping experience with Him.

When the Lights Go Out

One weekend, Matt and I took a quick business trip from our home in central Ohio to my hometown in West Virginia. We couldn't leave until after Matt got home from work Friday evening, so darkness had fallen before we arrived at my brother's house to spend the night. He lives in the country on the edge of a national forest, with a gate off the main road barring the long drive to his house. A very wet, sleety kind of snow had started to stream down, and the wind had picked up by the time we reached his beautiful, secluded property. We pulled into the entryway just in front of a locked gate. Matt hopped out to unlock the gate—but the instructions we'd been given didn't work. We were out of range of cell phone service, so we had to drive back into town and wake my brother with a phone call. I explained our dilemma, but he reiterated the steps we had already tried before. We had no choice but to try again.

There were no streetlights in sight as Matt drove through the sleet and snow to arrive at the gate a second time. Once again, we tried everything we knew to get it open, but nothing worked. The bolts were rusted from exposure to the elements. There was no way to drive across the bridge that night.

That bridge, by the way, was several decades old and had been built without side rails. We decided we would carry what we needed for the night across it and leave the car where it was. So we began to trek carefully across the slippery wooden slats, hearing nothing but the rushing water below our feet and feeling the cold sleet hitting our faces. When we reached the middle of the bridge, the automatic lights inside the car suddenly went out. The darkness was so thick that we stopped dead in our tracks, and with one voice exclaimed, "Whoa!" Without lights and a cloudy night sky, we couldn't see anything at all for a moment or two until Matt grabbed his phone and turned on the light. That little speck of dawn was enough to help us get across the bridge and show us the way to the door of my brother's home.

When we left for that trip, we thought we knew the way. We'd driven that road countless times. We owned phones with GPS maps built into them and used them. But nothing thoroughly prepared us for that moment when the lights went out and everything grew dark. The only thing I could say to my honey was, "Show me the way." I trusted him fully.

The next morning, when we could see the full view of the space we had walked across, we had to laugh at ourselves. It was not as scary as it had seemed in the pitch dark.

No matter how dark life gets, the Light of the world shines bright. When things get dark, ask for a little more light, a little more healing, another glimpse of His love. You need enough to keep walking until one day, the morning will come, sunlight will stream in, and you'll laugh as you look back at the spiritual forest you had such trouble seeing in the moments you were walking through it.

God, Show Me

God, give me a fresh vision to see things as You see them. While my humanity limits my earthly eyesight, I need a holy, supernatural perspective. Let prayer rule my heart so effectively that I never let the trees block my view of the spiritual forest of Your plan.

Chapter Ten Prayer Principles

- Look up in prayer, and you might discover a fresh way out of your circumstances.

- Praying for God to guide is asking for direction while praying for God to show up is asking for revelation.

- When we show up, God often shows off.

- Prayer reveals possibilities we didn't know existed, exposes provisions we couldn't predict, and demonstrates the power we wouldn't otherwise experience.

CHAPTER ELEVEN

Hello, I'm over Here

God, Remember Me.

A few years ago, my friend Jessica was "dirt poor and in the thick of raising babies," as she liked to say. One day, she lost her keys, including the expensive electronic key to her car. Her family turned the house inside out and upside down looking for it but could not find it.

When Jessica and her husband decided to replace the key, they were told it would cost almost a thousand dollars! And that didn't include towing the car to the shop to have the key remade. She was desperate, discouraged, and feeling loads of guilt. The following day, she collapsed on the front porch and cried, "God, please help me remember where I put the keys!" When she opened her eyes, the car keys were lying on the chair beside her, where she had tossed them the week before.

What a beautiful prayer story! In Jessica's mind, the keys were lost, but God knew where they were all along. She couldn't recall what she had done with them until, out of sheer desperation, she stopped to pray. As we've seen throughout this book, prayer is the catalyst for what was once lost to be found.

But what happens when praying desperately gives others the impression you've lost your mind?

Misunderstood and Misjudged

There is hardly a woman in the Bible who was more desperate than Hannah. Year after year, she grieved her barrenness. While her husband's love for her was so deep that he considered her his reason to breathe, Hannah could not fulfill her cultural role in their home by giving him a child. Meanwhile, Elkanah's second wife, Peninah, mocked her for her infertility. After having her fill of taunts, Hannah succumbed to full-blown anxiety.

Hannah lost her appetite and wouldn't eat, or perhaps couldn't. Even Elkanah grew exasperated with her, as his lavish doting failed to meet her emotional needs. At the peak of exasperation, he fired four questions at her: "Hannah, why are you weeping? Why don't you eat? Why are you downhearted? Don't I mean more to you than ten sons?" While the Bible doesn't describe his tone of voice, we can sense his frustration through his questions. *Why? Why? Why?*

If you've ever failed to ease someone else's sorrow, then you know Elkanah's response to Hannah at this point wasn't precisely well thought out.

The Bible tells us what Hannah did next: "In her deep anguish Hannah prayed to the Lord, weeping bitterly" (1 Samuel 1:10). The Hebrew words for "weeping bitterly" are the same for both "weeping" and "bitterly," and help us understand that she wept and then wept some more. And some more.

An editor once told me that I write about crying too much. That's almost as harsh as being told you actually cry too much. Most of us know that doesn't help us stop crying. If you are feeling such despair that weeping is all you can do, turning to God is the best place to take your tears. I've learned this the hard way. Hannah knew this, too.

But in this place of deep sorrow, Hannah's prayer silently made it to her lips. Imagine her praying in the Temple, distraught, and crying out to her God without making a sound. If you've been there yourself, it's easy to imagine. However, the casual observer might have glanced at her and moved away from "the crazy woman." Even Eli, the priest, thought she was drunk, and he scolded her.

If I were Hannah, I might have snapped at that moment. But she didn't. She had been wholly misjudged, adding insult to injury, but she didn't retaliate. She said,

I am a woman who is deeply troubled. I have not been drinking wine or beer; I was pouring out my soul to the

Lord. Do not take your servant for a wicked woman; I
have been praying here out of my great anguish and grief.
(1 Samuel 1:15–16)

At first glance, true prayer warriors may appear radical or
fanatical to the world or even to fellow Christians. But Hannah
was not satisfied to continue living in her state of grief. She
relinquished every care, concern, worry, and problem to her
great God. She wasn't ashamed to pour out her soul to the
Lord; she stood her ground and said that prayer was the best
tool in her arsenal for the intense war being waged against her.
Perhaps the psalmist's words echoed in her mind:

As the deer pants for streams of water, so my soul pants
for you, my God. My soul thirsts for God, for the living
God. When can I go and meet with God? My tears have
been my food day and night while people say to me all
day long, "Where is your God?" These things I remember
as I pour out my soul: how I used to go to the house of
God under the protection of the Mighty One with shouts
of joy and praise among the festive throng. (Psalm
42:1–4)

Hannah is a beautiful example of this humble attitude and
reminds us how we should pray. I feel like she "prays it forward." My friend and literary agent, Mary DeMuth, writes,

Even if friends or family members malign you, or strangers on social media threaten to expose you according to their prejudice, you can keep walking forward. . . .[1]

Although we cannot hear the tone of Hannah's voice, we can see Eli's change of heart in his response to her: "Go in peace, and may the God of Israel grant you what you have asked of him."

What did Hannah ask of God? She first asked, "God, look on me and remember me." Hannah's prayer was bold. Like Hagar, who we studied previously, she wanted God to see her and her problem. Also, she wanted God to see her pain and to do something about it. She wanted God to remember her.

The Hebrew word translated as "remember" used in 1 Samuel 1:11 somewhat limits our understanding of Hannah's request. She asked not only for the shame of infertility to be removed, but for God to move beyond it: She longed to be made into a memorial. She wanted her situation to be not only reversed but redeemed. "God, make me a trophy of Your glory" is what her "God, remember me" prayer truly meant.

Then, she moved further by attaching a purpose to her request. If God gave her a child, she planned to give him back. Her invocation of remembrance included God's purpose and plan. Peace flooded her heart and soul upon surrender.

> "God, make me a trophy of Your glory" is what her "God, remember me" prayer truly meant.

Remember That Scent

One beautiful spring day, a friend of mine buried his dear father after watching him fight cancer for many years. He told me that after walking away from his father's grave, he felt hope for the first time in a long time. Hope sometimes wears strange clothing, but Heaven seemed so near at that moment that he could almost touch it. The sun shone brightly that day, and weeks of spring rains had left the ground soft and green, and the smell of fresh-cut grass lingered in the air. Despite his deep grief, somehow, new life seemed to be on the horizon.

A decade later, my friend was driving through the country on another glorious spring day. But when he rolled down the car windows, he suddenly began to sob so fiercely that he was forced to pull over. The smell of spring mixed with fresh-cut grass took him back to the day he had buried his father.

Scents prompt our memories like nothing else can. Our ability to smell surpasses our other senses due to its direct connection to the hippocampus, the brain's primary communication center. This intimate neurological connection explains the tight-knit correlation between our noses and our memories.

Did you know that a mother's sense of smell is so strong that she can tell whether a piece of clothing belongs to her child or someone else's? We know not to touch baby animals in the wild because their mothers' noses will reject their baby because the scent of our hands will make them think they don't belong to them.

If this seems a little challenging to grasp, follow me for a minute.

In Exodus 30, God gave Moses and Aaron instructions for building the Tabernacle, where He would dwell among His people. Specific instructions included the priest's adding specially formulated incense when the lamps were tended each morning and evening. The priests themselves were to be anointed with a special oil that could not be poured on anyone else (Exodus 30:32). The perfume was sacred, and anyone using it who wasn't a priest would be cut off from his family. The oil poured over the priests was also used to anoint the Tabernacle meeting tent and each piece of furniture that God had instructed them to make for it. Then God commanded that a third mixture of fragrant spices be blended into a most holy incense. This powder would be purified with salt and placed in front of the Ark of the Covenant, where God would meet with Moses. This third incense also would be considered holy to the Lord, and whoever made it to enjoy on their own would be cut off from their people.

Each of the three incense blends served a specific purpose and signified a relationship. The lamps at the Tabernacle entrance emitted a scent that welcomed those who entered, signaling that God longs to welcome us into His presence. That scent beckoned to Hannah even before she arrived at the entryway when she went to worship. Her prayers joined the inviting smoke God had uniquely crafted to signify an opportunity to commune with Him. As her words united with the specially scented perfume, God enjoyed *her* scent—that of the one He knew and loved. Maybe He said to Himself, "I see you, My child. I recognize the essence of My children, and you belong to Me." Perhaps the words of the psalmist reverberated in Hannah's mind,

> I call to you, Lord, come quickly to me; hear me when I call to you. May my prayer be set before you like incense; may the lifting up of my hands be like the evening sacrifice. (Psalm 141:2)

As Eli reprimanded her, surely Hannah smelled his anointing oil. Maybe the scent that set him apart from others was the very thing that kept her spirit humble as she responded to his words. His "cologne" reminded her that she stood before God's anointed one and that his words should not be taken lightly; then his affirming message of peace over her prayer and his spoken blessing over her request anchored her heart in hope. She could eat! Her face was no longer sad. Although her answer had not yet come, Hannah's attitude was transformed. After pouring out the bitterness of her soul, requesting her heart's desire, and humbling herself to embrace God's plan, she worshiped the Lord and returned home.

Next, 1 Samuel 1:19 tells us, "Elkanah made love to his wife Hannah, and the Lord remembered her." The Hebrew expression that "the Lord remembers" someone does not mean that God had previously forgotten that person, but that He has intervened favorably after a time of silence. In some languages, it would be appropriate to translate that phrase as "bear me in mind."[2] God certainly chose to make a memorial of Hannah. The thing that brought her the most profound grief was the very thing that brought her closest to God. Desperation for God transforms beautifully into dependence on God. Total dependence on God is precisely where our loving Father wants us to live.

> *Desperation for God transforms beautifully into dependence on God.*

When God gave Hannah the desire of her heart—a son named Samuel—she gave it back to God. Samuel's name means "asked of God." Hannah is the only woman named in the Bible who is described as making a vow to God that she kept.

Imagine the day Hannah returned to Shiloh to return her son to God. My heart can hardly comprehend the strength it must have taken to honor her promise to the Lord. As she moved toward the tabernacle gate, the welcoming incense likely reminded her of her previous visit, when she had asked God to remember her.

Hannah's greeting to Eli may have gone something like this: "Remember me? Remember how you told me God would answer my prayer? Well, here's the answer." Then Samuel stepped forward. God delights in answering the impossible prayers of His children.

Memory-Making Prayers

Years ago, my sister gave me a beautiful treasure box. It has a cherry finish and a photo of my dear mom on the lid, so only the most cherished, meaningful objects earn a storage place inside—including handwritten letters from my mom. Even more than twenty years after her graduation to Heaven, I occasionally open the box to recall her love for me. I never want to forget how much she loved me and how I long for the day when we will be reunited. I don't want to let time fade the memory of our deep connection, though, in my humanity, this could happen if I allowed it.

God treasures your prayers so much that He stores them carefully. Your prayers, the essence of communication with your Creator, are so precious that He holds them carefully for safekeeping. Revelation 5:8 illustrates this:

> And when he had taken it, the four living creatures and the twenty-four elders fell down before the Lamb. Each one had a harp, and they were holding golden bowls full of incense, which are the prayers of God's people.

Each prayer carries a unique scent, an identifier that only God, the master perfumer, knows. Collectively, the glorious scent of prayer is infused with unity that can only be interpreted by God the Father.

> *Each prayer carries a unique scent, an identifier that only God, the master perfumer, knows.*

When each of my kiddos started kindergarten, I wanted to sit on the couch with a tissue box and a tub of ice cream while looking through their baby books. At the end of 1 Samuel 1, Hannah left her Samuel at the Tabernacle under Eli's care, and one would naturally think that, as a mother, she would react the same way I did on kindergarten day.

But Chapter 2 begins with Hannah praying again. Yes, again. She is the only woman in the Bible to have two recorded prayers. A paraphrase of the first five verses of her prayer might read like this: "I'm not afraid to talk about what God has done for me. There is no one like Him; His holiness and strength exceed anyone else's. God's hand has weakened the strong and strengthened the weak. God has the ultimate power of reversal." Hannah's first prayer is a plea of desperation; her second is a song of praise. Her first ached with sorrow; her second overflowed with joy. Her first prayer is one verse long; her second is ten.

Hannah's prayer of praise thanks God for salvation, security, sovereignty, sustenance, supernatural power, supremacy, settlement, safeguarding, and strength. I can hardly fathom how precious this prayer of praise must have been to her and her loving Heavenly Father.

I deeply appreciate her statement towards the end of the prayer in 1 Samuel 2:9: "It is not by strength that one prevails. . . ." Hannah couldn't pull herself up by her sandal straps. She had no power to change her situation. But our weakest prayerful pleas to God are the beginning of our strongest moments.

More than once, I have had to figure out what life looks like without my loved ones living in this world. But the worst

> *Our weakest prayerful pleas to God are the beginning of our strongest moments.*

suffering we endured together carved a path to Jesus's feet, and I have realized that is the only place I ever want to be.

In my prayer time this morning, I began with a full confession: "Lord, I'm a hot mess." I felt His reply: "Girl, you're catching on."

A few moments later, I grabbed my shoes from the closet, only to glimpse Taylor's winter coat hanging there. The bright pink often catches my eye. I pressed my face into the sleeve to breathe in the scent of my precious girl, which still lingers there. Although the earthly smell will fade with time, I soaked it up in the moment, knowing that God remembers both of us. Our story is being made into a memorial; He's not finished yet. For this, I whisper, "Thank you, Lord," and send the incense of praise to the heavens, anticipating the day when Taylor and I can breathe in each other's scent once again.

God, Remember Me

God, I feel lost and need Your divine help. May the scent of this prayer permeate Your throne room and remind You of my deep desire to be remembered. Make this prayer the fresh beginning of total reliance on You. Please make a memorial of my life.

Chapter Eleven Prayer Principles

- Prayer is the catalyst for what was once lost to be found.
- If you are feeling such despair that weeping is all you can do, turning to God in the midst of deep sorrow is the best thing to do with the tears.
- Desperation for God transforms beautifully into dependence on God.
- Our weakest prayerful pleas to God are the beginning of our strongest moments.

CHAPTER TWELVE

Miracles Happen

God, Wow Me.

It's easy to get stuck when your miracle doesn't happen your way or on your timetable. You're inundated with messages telling you that you *deserve* to have things your way. Why couldn't your mom experience healing from cancer? Why did your friend have to die? Why didn't God heal my precious Taylor and bring the miracle of life into her body? Most of us have asked God for a miracle at least once in our lives, right? Probably more than once.

Being thankful after Taylor died seemed unfathomable. When I finally could scrape together a few words to pray, I sometimes would whisper, "God, wow me." To me, that request was asking God to bring a little surprise element to the day. I wanted Him to do something that would make me smile and let me know that He loved me. Something that would help me see that He was near, no matter how far away He seemed. I wasn't looking for anything enormous by using the word "wow." It was about experiencing a God moment, one in which even the surprise and delight of a beautiful flower or simple cup of tea could usher in gratitude.

My expectations were about specific, small circumstances that I knew only God could orchestrate. Honestly, larger-than-life miracles seemed less probable in that season of my grief journey. Though I still believed God was bigger than anything, my hurting heart struggled to process all my questions of *why*.

I'm guessing you've been there. Perhaps you say you believe in God, but you still keep Him in a box. We sometimes conclude that God has limits because we've experienced limitations in our prayers. We stop asking God for "big things" because we forget that He wants to do "more than we can ask or imagine" (Ephesians 3:20).

> *We sometimes conclude that God has limits because we've experienced limitations in our prayers.*

Never Been a Day Like It

"The Sun Stands Still." This chapter heading in the book of Joshua has always stood out to me. There was a day when the sun literally stopped moving—and doesn't that mean that the earth must have stopped spinning? It's challenging to think that the earth would literally stand still because of one man's prayer, yet that is precisely what happened.

As the appointed leader to the nation of Israel, Joshua stepped into big shoes when Moses died. Yet his profound faith in God was one of the reasons he was chosen for this role. Joshua 10 shows us Joshua leading his men through battle after battle. After they destroyed Ai, the leaders of the royal city of Gibeon struck a treaty with Israel. Because of these two events, five wicked kings throughout Canaan came together to attack Gibeon, which appealed to Joshua for urgent assistance. Facing five armies at once would be completely insane, yet God spoke directly to Joshua about it.

"Do not be afraid of them; I have given them into your hand. Not one of them will be able to withstand you." (Joshua 10:8)

I think it's easy to look at words in the Bible like God's promise above and think, *Of course. God promised. Said and done.* But let's station ourselves in Joshua's place for a moment.

This trip from Gilgal, where Joshua and his men were staying, to Gibeon, where the five kings and their armies camped, wasn't a short drive to Grandma's house. It was an all-night march to the battlefield. However, Joshua's attack surprised the five kings and their armies, and the Lord confused them. This supernatural turmoil set the kings on the run, with Israel pursuing them. God also hurled hailstones from the sky, and more of the enemy was killed by hail than by the Israelites' swords. At some point, amid the confusion, Joshua stopped and prayed in front of his entire army.

I heard all sorts of prayers in church while I was growing up. When I was only five or six years old, I would attend Saturday evening prayer meetings with my dad. A few people would gather—maybe a dozen—and most of them had white hair. Or no hair. Their wrinkles appeared almost crunchy to my five-year-old eyes, and their prayers were long. I can still hear their words, pleading for God to use the church to reach the community. Then they would pray over the lists of names of people with needs: Susie needed healing from a fall. Johnny's parents desired for him to return home safely from the military. Most of the prayers I heard in that small-town church were quiet yet passionate.

By contrast, prayers in the formal church services seemed to follow the formula of "the louder, the better." Usually, there was no microphone for the usher praying before the offering or the deacon asked to close the service, so a slight yell was deemed necessary. Those prayers contained words that would give the average person pause today. Words like "thee" and "thou" were prevalent. A certain pontificating quality seemed to be a requirement. The more "Our Fathers" inserted, the more critical the prayer—or at least so it seemed to me.

So when I imagine Joshua standing before his men, calling all to attention in prayer, I feel that his sense of urgency was like that of the sweet folks in the prayer room, but his volume equaled the deacons'. I know one thing: This pause for prayer was pivotal in that battle.

Joshua called out for something more significant than I could imagine or think:

> Joshua said to the Lord in the presence of Israel: "Sun, stand still over Gibeon, and you, moon, over the Valley of Aijalon." (Joshua 10:12)

The wording in this passage explains that Joshua was talking to God, the sun, and the moon at the same time. He addressed the sun and moon with his mouth, but his heart addressed the One who held the sun and moon in orbit and, therefore, could hold the sun and moon in place. He was using his God-given authority over creation to legislate something specific to happen in the natural realm.

What a prayer for a miracle within a miracle! God had already promised Joshua the miracle of winning the battle against incredible odds. But Joshua implored God not to back down, to finish what had been started, and to ask for additional help. He prayed for the impossible. And then:

> The sun stopped in the middle of the sky and delayed going down about a full day. There has never been a day like it before or since when the Lord listened to a human

being. Surely the Lord was fighting for Israel! (Joshua 10:13–14)

(I can't help but fall in love with that exclamation point.)

The victory inched so close that Joshua didn't want the day to end, so God pressed the pause button on the planetary orbits to usher in the miracle he needed. No other day in history has ever doubled in hours. There's never been another day when the Lord heard human words and honored them in this way.

Joshua could have complained when the Gibeonites called on him for assistance. He could have asked, "Where's my miracle?"—especially when his men had to march all night to begin fighting. But what he certainly couldn't miss was that God heard him, listened to him, and ushered in the miracle. His "God, wow me" prayer was answered miraculously.

God is not bound by time. His power exceeds our requests or imagination. Still, I have to imagine He was thinking, "Wow, good one, Joshua. Let's do this thing!"

Sometimes we don't recognize the miracle God is working on our behalf because we've missed the invitation to engage with Him in the process. We're so busy complaining about not getting the blessing we wanted that we fail to

> *Sometimes we don't recognize the miracle God is working on our behalf because we've missed the invitation to engage with Him in the process.*

see the opportunity to be a part of any miracle He wants to perform on our behalf. God wants to "wow" you; maybe your "wow me" moment lies just ahead.

Didn't See That Coming

Several months before Taylor took a final turn for the worse, a woman I barely knew called me for help. She also had an adult child she cared for at home. The expenses and weight of the physical demands had exhausted her family, and she desperately needed daily assistance. She knew I had been walking the caregiving path for many years and asked for my advice on her options.

I wanted to help her, but I wasn't sure if the opportunities would be the same for her son as for my Taylor, so I started to research the government programs available. In the process, I stumbled upon a federal tax regulation that I hadn't seen or heard of before which said the tax dollars paid to caregivers for disabled adult children through specific funding programs are not taxable wages. I asked my accountant to research the regulation and see if we needed to make any changes—but then got so caught up with caring for Taylor and the rest of my family that I forgot about it.

A few months passed, and so did my precious girl. For a while, I became a hermit. Loss makes you want to hole up in a cave. But for me, corporate worship is a necessary thread in my life fabric. I need it like I need water to live. So only a week after my daughter's lifeless body was placed in the cold, hard ground, I was sitting in church while my husband prepared to sing with the worship team. Part of me wished I could disappear, but another part knew how much I needed to be there.

Our accountant glanced back from the row where he sat beside his wife, then stood and walked down the aisle to talk to me. I tried to slow my jumbled thoughts down long enough to be sensible. Any question would seem like a hard one.

He sat down and asked, "How are you?"

I replied, "The best I can be under the circumstances."

"I understand," he said, nodding. "I have something to share with you."

He had been unaware of the regulation I had emailed him about, and said we needed to file amended returns so that the money I had inadvertently paid could be refunded. Over the last three years, I had overpaid thousands of dollars in state and federal taxes.

Having that back would give us enough money to help us do something we had only dreamed of up to that point: remodeling our house or moving into a larger home. The house where our family of eight had lived for seventeen years held many great memories, but parts of it brought more challenge than convenience. The kitchen was small, and the pantry was unworthy of its name. A few canned goods and lunch items, along with the broom and dustpan, were all its narrow shelves could hold. The laundry room was in the bowels of the basement, which meant every sheet, towel, blanket, and piece of clothing had to be carted up and down two flights of stairs. We usually made a game of throwing our dirty laundry down the steps, but toting the heavy baskets filled with folded laundry was a daily task that often cut into my family and work time. Balancing time and money is quite the juggling act for large families. (I call it "large family logistics.")

We had plenty of square footage to work with, but the floor plan was mostly chopped up into small sections. When our children were small, their belongings were small—but now that they were teenagers and young adults with adult-sized clothings and shoes, finding space was a struggle. We had two dining rooms, but one had carpet and could only be used for guests or special occasions, so we usually all crammed into the breakfast nook for every meal.

I didn't feel there was much we could do about it, as we strived to live as close to debt-free as possible. We believed in adhering to our budget, and although we had accumulated a lot of equity in our home, there was no wiggle room to save for the down payment on a larger house. That would take a miracle or drastic change in circumstances, and Matt and I both knew it.

But on this seemingly random Sunday, through a situation I never would have dreamed of, God completely wowed us. Eleven months later, we moved into a brand-new home. God had done more than we could ask or imagine—a miracle from Heaven that only He could provide.

When I whispered, "God, wow me," I was thinking about a flower or cup of tea—but God had something much more extraordinary in store for me and my family.

God in a Box, Please

Sometimes, we shove God in a box without even realizing it. Then we place the lid firmly on that box by believing that the way we imagine He will answer our prayer is the only way that will work. We might even tie a pretty bow around the box to make it look like we have our act together and use that bow as a reminder that our way is best. In our humanity, we may not intend to limit God, but our minds aren't capable of grasping the whole picture of our lives and how today fits into eternity. Even the shrewdest intellectuals of our age aren't capable of thinking higher than the Creator of the Universe does.

As He has reminded us,

"For my thoughts are not your thoughts, neither are your ways my ways," declares the Lord. "For as the heavens are higher than the earth, so are my ways higher than your ways and my thoughts than your thoughts." (Isaiah 55:8)

I can't wrap my head around the intricacy of God's plan for the entire world. So when I go to Him in prayer with my "agenda," I'm sure if I were Him, I'd be shaking My head at me. While He loves to hear my voice and listen to my heart, He wants to give me even more than I ask Him for.

Doesn't it seem strange to be afraid to ask God for too much? It's as if we think we are standing in line at the school cafeteria, and God dollops a spoonful of potatoes on our tray. We love mashed potatoes and want to ask for more—but potatoes are starch and can't be too good for a person. But God doesn't think the way we do. When I ask for more mashed potatoes, He says, "Girl, I've not only got your mashed potatoes, I'll give you a whole plate of them if you're that hungry. And I know you love gravy. Yep—get yourself some gravy. That gravy is better than any you've ever tasted before."

God's plan for your life surpasses your creativity. God's plan for you exceeds your logical ability to request it from Him, and you can't even begin to imagine what He has in store for you.

> *God's plan for your life surpasses your creativity.*

So go ahead. Love Him. Ask for a wow moment. Pray bigger. Maybe you'll catch a few extra rays of sunshine or break history and enjoy an entire extra day of it.

God, Wow Me

God, I've placed You in a box of my design. Take the ribbon, Lord, and make something of my current circumstances that exceeds my request. Ditch my ideas that aren't Yours, but whatever You do, Lord, move beyond my limited imagination. God, wow me.

Chapter Twelve Prayer Principles

- Sometimes we don't recognize the miracle God is working on our behalf because we've missed the invitation to engage with Him in the process.
- God longs to "wow" you; maybe your "wow me" moment lies just ahead.
- Sometimes, we box God in and limit Him in our prayers.
- God's plan for your life surpasses your creativity.

CHAPTER THIRTEEN

Out of the Pit

God, Free Me.

"But, Mommy, there's a monster under the bed!" Many parents have heard their child give that stereotypical reason for refusing to return to their own room after crawling into bed with you in the middle of the night. When I was eight, the "monster" was a gorilla chasing me. Mind you, I'd never visited a city zoo and had only seen a photo of a gorilla. But in my mind, that shiny, excited gorilla chased me around my childhood home until I was exhausted. When I collapsed on the couch, it sat on top of me, and I couldn't breathe. Just when I felt like I was blacking out, I would jerk awake with a gasp. The feeling of suffocation was so real that my chest still tightens as I write this.

If I can still feel the effects of an inexplicable childhood dream, imagine what Jonah must have felt while he was literally trapped in the belly of a whale.

I'm guessing you may have heard of this famous character, well-known for his three-night stay in an unestablished WaterBnB. Jonah's story is limited to just four chapters in the Bible, yet the idea of living inside a big fish has grabbed the attention of young and old alike for thousands of years. Famous pieces of art, from paintings to sculptures, have been created to depict his predicament; we are fascinated by it because the story is too large for our minds to fathom.

The beginning of the book that Jonah most likely wrote himself[1] shows us that God commanded him to go to the city of Nineveh and preach against the wickedness of the people who lived there. "But Jonah ran away from the Lord and headed for Tarshish" (Jonah 1:3).

Have you ever had a "but" in your life? A time when the godly people surrounding you gave their advice, but you ignored them to follow the "but"? The time you knew the Holy Spirit was speaking to your heart to do something specific, but you pushed it out of your mind, away from your heart, and went your own way? I have, and y'all, it's painful. The "but" is painful enough when God directs you one way and you obstinately choose to stay right where you are—but it's even more painful when you not only tell God you aren't moving in His direction, but you turn around and run the opposite way. That's rebellion. And rebellious Jonah was definitely on the run.

God's journey for Jonah was about 500 miles long, but Jonah's plan was 2,500 miles long—all the way from ancient Israel to Tarshish, located in modern-day Spain.² After he paid for his ticket on the ship from Joppa, I like to imagine he stood on the deck for a while, letting the wind blow through his beard, looking back to the shore, and thinking about how this had to be better than what God had told him to do. Friend, you can run from God, but expect to be lovingly pursued.

While Jonah slept in a cabin below deck, the Lord blew in a storm that threatened to rip the ship to shreds. All the sailors, newbie and veteran alike, feared for their lives, throwing off the cargo to lighten the load and keep from sinking. Each one called on the gods they worshiped, begging for their lives. At that point, the captain woke up Jonah.

How in the world was Jonah sleeping through that storm? It's easy to ask that—but have you ever lulled yourself into a daze because you wanted to ignore what was right in front of your face? I have. This is why grief makes it hard to get out of bed. This is why harsh circumstances are sometimes what it takes to challenge us to move forward. It's easier to numb ourselves and block out the consequences of our choices than it is to face them, whether those choices are in the past, present, or future. So I feel for what Jonah must have been going through at that moment.

But God didn't leave him alone in the bottom of that boat, trying to numb his heart and block out the world. He sent

someone to help him. The person he sent wasn't a fellow fol-
lower of God, but a worldly boat captain who shook Jonah and
told him exactly what he should do. "Pray, man, pray!" He
compelled Jonah to call out to his God for help.

Let's stop right here to get this. A sea captain who trusted
in pagan gods commanded Jonah, God's prophet, to pray in
that life-or-death situation. And there is no record of Jonah's
doing so at that moment.

When I get to Heaven, I plan to ask Jonah why he didn't
pray right then and there. He could have saved everyone a *lot*
of trouble. But I guess Jonah had at least two reasons: First, he
felt guilty. After all, he actually was to blame for that storm,
and he knew it. How could he go to God in prayer when his
choice had prompted that disaster? Shame, guilt, and blame are
tools the enemy uses to keep us from calling out to God. If he
can make us think the fault is all ours *and* that God doesn't
want to hear from us, then he's won the battle.

Secondly, I'm guessing that Jonah was still angry with God.
He didn't want to be the one to go to Nineveh. He didn't want
to use his time and energy to preach to heathens. He had absolutely zero desire to face the persecution the Ninevites would
likely wreak upon him. He writes later that he wanted God to
consume the Ninevites in His wrath rather than flood them
with His mercy; he'd already judged them in his own heart and
wasn't approaching the situation with God's compassion. So he
held his ground against the Lord God Almighty, whom he knew
and had previously served. Instead, he chose the stubborn stance.
By then, humbling himself in prayer was far from his mind.

At that point, the sailors resorted to casting lots, essentially letting the luck of the dice reveal who was to blame for the storm. The lot correctly fell on Jonah, who revealed his identity. He had already told the crew he was running from God, but when he revealed that his God was the One who made the sea and dry land, the crew was terrified.

They desperately asked Jonah what to do. This could have served as the prompt for Jonah to pray. When I read this story in the Bible, I want to yell out, "Just ask God to calm the storm! You know He is merciful. Fall to your knees and tell Him you know He's the one chasing you!" But still, Jonah did not pray. Instead, he told the men to throw him overboard. He would rather face death than surrender to the One who controlled the storm.

I wish Jonah's heart hadn't been so hardened, that he could have seen that God's plan held so much more for him. I wonder what caused him to be so legalistic and bitter.

The captain did his best to avoid that drastic measure, trying to get his team and row the ship back to shore, but the wild waves only raged higher. Ultimately, the men who did not know God personally were the ones who cried out to Him.

"Please, Lord, do not let us die for taking this man's life. Do not hold us accountable for killing an innocent man, for you, Lord, have done as you pleased." Then they took Jonah and threw him overboard, and the raging sea grew calm. (Jonah 1:14–15)

After all they had witnessed, these men turned their worship from the gods they had known to the God who knew them. What they saw God do changed their hearts and what they believed about Him.

> *Storms can either prevent or prompt prayer; we get to choose between those options.*

Storms can either prevent or prompt prayer; we get to choose between those options.

The Many Faces of Rebellion

Twice in my life, I rebelled against God. The average person who observed me might not even be able to tell that I was angry at Him and harboring bitterness at the time. I didn't drive 100 miles per hour with rock music blaring. I didn't suddenly make swearing, smoking, and drinking part of my lifestyle. But I am here to tell you that my heart had issues. Major ones.

I was running as far away from God as I could get. My prayer life was nonexistent. I didn't want to talk to God because I blamed Him for my circumstances. Why did my ex-husband choose to leave me for another woman? Why did my dreams of having a family get crushed? Why did God trust me with a child whose life expectancy was only ten to fifteen years? Anger and bitterness festered like open sores over the life I was living versus the one I had dreamed of. (If you read my book *One More Step: Finding Strength When You Feel Like Giving Up*, you'll discover how I learned to accept God's forgiveness and to forgive others and how pivotal that lesson was for me.)

My second season of strong rebellion was similar to Jonah's. I was serving the Lord through blogging, freelance writing for magazines, writing books, and speaking at events. Our family relied on Matt's full-time job to pay the bills while I supplemented our income in this way—but then Matt lost his job. For the first few months, I held fast to faith in God's timing. But as time marched on, I began to fight the urge to run away from God daily. I looked at online job postings, thinking that maybe God hadn't called me into the publishing world after all. Every form of work I performed was related to ministry, and none of it paid enough to meet our family's financial needs. Logically, getting what I often called "a real job" made the most sense. Matt would have to talk me off the ledge of applying for jobs in places where I didn't belong. I was fighting a war in my heart, and I had to start every day on the floor, begging God to show me what to do, asking Him for wisdom, and relying on Him.

There was nothing wrong with Tarshish, mind you. God said nothing against the place Jonah chose to run, and He had nothing against any of the businesses where I was tempted to apply for jobs. The storm wasn't stirred up by *where* Jonah was running; God designed it to make Jonah aware of *Who* he was running from. The financial storm in our family's life was designed to draw us closer to our God in deeper relationship. It was an opportunity to learn how to discern His voice and then fully obey Him. I journaled my prayers daily in that season, and one of them reads:

*God, I surrender my life, my husband, my children, our
home, and my all to You. I love You, Jesus. Let the work
of my hands be profitable for You alone. Show me how
to live today, Father. Guide me, Holy Spirit. Jesus, You
are holy. I trust in You. I lift myself to You. I give myself
to You. I am Your servant.*

There is nothing eloquent about the words in that prayer. When
I read it now, I can feel the urgency within those short, chopped-
off phrases. Desperation, indeed. I wrote out many Bible verses
in that season, but Psalm 86:7 was especially poignant: "When
I am in distress, I call to you, because you answer me."

Another entry ends: "I am desperate, Jesus. Let it be for
You." Remember how I mentioned earlier that desperation for
God promotes dependence on God?

I know that storm you are facing is a struggle. I can see
those waves expanding and threatening to take down your
ship. The One who controls the sea chases after you and me;
He is our Captain.

Untangling Seaweed

Jonah was thrown overboard, but that's certainly not where his
story ends. God had prepared a huge fish to swallow him, and
he languished in the belly of the whale for three days and three
nights. He had wished himself dead, but God had intervened.
There was only one thing left to do, so he prayed. (Finally!)

He said: "In my distress I called to the Lord, and he answered me. From deep in the realm of the dead I called for help, and you listened to my cry." (Jonah 2:2)

Does this sound familiar? Jonah's prayer echoes the psalmist's in the same way my prayers did. Why did it take three days and three nights for Jonah to finally pray? Maybe he thought that God couldn't see him because he couldn't see God. The water had engulfed him. Seaweed was wrapped around his head, covering his eyes. It wasn't necessarily about the seaweed, though; Jonah needed to be freed from himself. His own selfish ideals and plans needed to be washed out to sea, never to return.

Recently I learned that whales typically don't hug shorelines because they know the danger of getting stuck in shallow water. Clearly God was listening for Jonah's cry, and upon hearing it, He acted on his behalf. He answered Jonah's prayer by causing the whale to vomit Jonah out onto dry land—not in the deep water where Jonah would have been forced to swim to shore, nor in choppy waves or in a riptide. No, God specifically positioned Jonah's drop-off at the best possible location for someone with seaweed wrapped around his head.

If I could sum up his lengthy prayer in Jonah 2, it would be: *God, free me. Free me from thinking that I have it all figured out.*

> *When we come to the end of ourselves, we find God and the true freedom to experience the life He longs to provide.*

Free me from forgetting that Your ways are higher. Free me from the decisions I've made that have resulted in poor circumstances. Free me to embrace the salvation that comes from You.

When we come to the end of ourselves, we find God and the true freedom to experience the life He longs to provide.

Free Indeed

My husband grew up in a Christian home similar to mine. His dad was a pastor and evangelist, serving in full-time ministry for more than fifty years. Meanwhile, Matt's mom was a full-time homemaker. When Matt was just four, he asked Jesus into his heart, and then, because he didn't remember his first salvation experience, he committed his life to Christ again at age ten. He wanted to be sure he was going to Heaven one day, and he longed to serve God with all his heart.

As a preacher's kid, he always knew a lot about Scripture. His dad would call him to the front of their church to recite the books of the Bible; he read through it several times as a child and teenager. His knowledge of the Bible far surpassed that of the average person, even those who grew up in church or studied advanced theology.

Biblical knowledge saturated Matt's head, but not his heart.

While attending a Christian university with the intention of becoming a doctor one day, Matt began dating a young lady whose family lived close to his own. They fell in love and married, then had a beautiful little girl together. Despite those blessings, Matt grew discouraged, partially because he didn't get accepted into the medical school he had chosen. So he settled into a part-time job at a hospital, where he met a woman who made him feel great about himself in areas where his confidence was lacking. She laughed at all his jokes and flirted in what some would call a harmless manner. Eventually, Matt became involved in an affair with her.

If you had told Matt as a teenager that he would wind up divorced one day, he would have said you were crazy, flat-out out of your mind. But that's where he landed. His choice to run from God included running from his marriage. For seven years, he lived a prodigal life, away from the Lord and the faith he had held onto as a child and teenager. The lifestyle he chose during those years is not one he is proud of today. His parents and siblings prayed continually that he would stop running in rebellion and turn back to the God who loved him so much.

After battling relational heartbreak and ending up more emotionally broken and fragile than he ever could have imagined, like Jonah, God sent Matt a sea captain of sorts: A nurse he was working with invited him to church, and that started a transition in his life. He turned to the Lord and wiped the seaweed from his eyes. Desperately, he cried out, and God placed him in a church community where the worship pastor told him he needed to start singing. Before then, Matt never knew that God had given him an incredible voice. Matt began to sing on the worship team, which provided him with community and accountability.

When I met Matt, he had been serving the Lord at that church for almost two years. I have never known the "Jonah" version of him and can't imagine the person he describes during those seven years. The seaweed was already cleaned up; the vomit was never to be seen again. I'm so thankful for the prayers of the people that preserved him and that he chose to cry out to God in his despair so that I could have a committed Christian husband and our redemption story could unfold in a way that could only be from God.

When you find yourself in the belly of despair or wrapped in the seaweed of confusion, God is always only a prayer away. He hears every whisper of your heart and every plea for His mercy. He can't wait to have the next conversation with you. What a glorious gift to walk in the freedom that He has planned for you!

God, Free Me

God, a part of my heart is tempted to run or has been running from You. Let this current storm prompt me to remember that You are ever pursuing me; You love me that much. Free me from the junk that threatens to tie me up. Set me free from obstacles so that I may praise Your name.

Chapter Thirteen Prayer Principles

- You can run from God, but expect to be lovingly pursued.
- Storms can prevent or prompt prayer. We get to choose between those options.
- The One who controls the sea chases after you and me.
- When we come to the end of ourselves, we find God.
- When we find ourselves in the belly of despair or wrapped in the seaweed of confusion, God is always only a prayer away.

I Need a Revival

God, Revive Me.

Second chances are special. There are just some things in life for which you don't get another try. As you can imagine after reading the story of my marriage to Matt, second chances are significant to both of us.

One of the ways we've intentionally nurtured God's gift of marriage is to spend our anniversary week someplace without our kiddos. While we love them beyond measure, we know one of the greatest blessings we can give them is parents who love each other well. Modeling that sometimes results in teenagers telling us to get a room when they see us kissing in the kitchen. (So we comply.)

Granted, that annual trip has required sacrifice over the years. We've had to make it work on a wing-and-a-prayer kind of budget. Our first stop on any trip is always the grocery store. Cooking meals costs much less than eating out at restaurants, so gourmet peanut butter and jelly sandwiches are often on the menu during our anniversary week.

For years, Matt and I visited the mountains for our anniversary, but later shifted to the beach—quite far from our home in Ohio. The rhythmic sound of ocean waves restores my soul like nothing else can. When I sit on the beach and stare at the blue sky reflected in the water, I'm amazed by our Creator. Those ocean waves feel like God's love is washing over me, and when grieving, the volume of water gives me the sense that God understands tears.

I exhaled fully when Matt and I sat down on the beach for the first time after our Taylor girl graduated to Heaven. After basking in the sunshine for a while, Matt was ready for one of those gourmet peanut butter and jelly sandwiches from our picnic basket. I passed one over to him, then unwrapped another for myself. I was preparing to take my first bite, when *whoosh!* Suddenly, the entire sandwich was snatched from my hand. It startled me so badly that it took another moment for me to realize that a bird had stolen my sandwich as his lunch!

All that preparation, time, and money had been invested, only to sit on the beach sandwichless. It's funny now, and of course, my kids love to think of a bird stealing Mom's sandwich right out of her hand. They also like to imitate my look of alarm. But y'all, sometimes restoration doesn't go according to plan.

Listening Ears On

I find the books in the section of the Bible labeled as being written by "minor prophets" fascinating. I've shared that I love a good underdog story; if the word "minor" doesn't indicate "underdog," I don't know what does. The writer in me empathizes with the minor prophets. Maybe they are the ones who missed the best-sellers lists of their time. (Kidding.) Seriously, the difference between the major and minor prophets is simply the number of chapters in each of their books; it's a quantitative label.

Habakkuk is one of the minor prophets who stands out in the prayer department. With only three chapters, his book is a conversation between him and God. Habakkuk didn't believe in mincing words; Habakkuk 1:2 begins, "How long, Lord, must I call for help, but you do not listen?" Ouch. Talk about starting on a sour note. However, God's response is filled with assurance. He explains that though times are tough and the city is under siege and filled with evil, His plan still prevails.

"Look at the nations and watch—and be utterly amazed. For I am going to do something in your days that you would not believe, even if you were told."

Sounds good, right? We would all tell Habakkuk to sit up and notice God's power. I'm sure someone would quote one of my favorite passages to him. "Habakkuk, trust in the Lord with all your heart. Do not lean on your own understanding."

But the prophet's response to God is a second complaint: *Why?* Why does the Sovereign God of the world let the enemy reign over it? If Habakkuk were living today, his question would likely be, *Why do bad things happen to good people?* He might further ask, *Why am I praying against the evil in the world if You aren't going to do anything about it, God?*

Can you feel his angst? I'm guessing you can. We all want to understand why prayer makes a difference if God isn't changing the situation we're praying about. Why even pray if God already has a plan? But prayer isn't only about the changes we can see with our eyes and hold in our hands. Prayer involves communing with our Creator and seeing hearts transformed—starting with our own. So like Habakkuk, when we pray, asking God to stop the evil or shift the situation, we surrender to his Sovereignty.

Habakkuk realized he was not in control; his job was to become aware of what God was doing. He was to focus on communication with the heavenly headquarters. So he chose to "stand at my watch and station myself on the ramparts." This stance was not a commanding battle position; his was a spot

> *Prayer involves communing with our Creator and seeing hearts transformed— starting with our own.*

from which to "look and listen." He chose to make prayer not only his complaint but also his concentration.

When my children were little and all talking at once, no one could hear what Mommy was saying. My voice is naturally relatively soft, and even when I tried to raise it, their collective voices were louder than mine. So I decided to say, "Oh, wait, guys, we need to put our listening ears on" whenever that happened. I would grab at the air in front of me with both hands and place each hand over my ear as if I were putting on headphones. Now that we had our listening ears on, we could stop talking over each other, and everyone could hear from me, the momma.

Habakkuk did the same thing. He stopped talking and stepped into his prayer tower, where he put his listening ears on. The prayer tower deepens our relationship with God. It's where we stop talking and start listening. It's where we clear our heads and calm our hearts by focusing on the truth of what God says about a matter, not the solution we hope to see. We pause to enjoy listening to God as much as we embrace talking to Him.

When I was taking Spanish in college, I knew a lot of words, but stringing them together in the proper format was a challenge. I would practice by asking the native speakers in my community how my Spanish sounded, and they would laugh and say, "Miss Racquel, you can say a lot of words, but you sound like a baby." My speech didn't equal mature conversation. The way to grow in communication skills was to continue practicing.

Many books are dedicated to the topic of learning how to listen to the voice of God. My skill in this is not professionally

honed by any means. If you asked, God might tell you I listen
like a baby. (Maybe someday I'll write a different book about
that.) But hearing God speak to our hearts requires a willingness to first step into the tower and put our listening ears on.
It's hard to hear His voice if we aren't considering what He
has to say through His Word, Spirit, and people. Recently I
prayed, "Lord, I want to be Holy Spirit led." He replied,
"Then you've got to be Holy Spirit fed." The feeding comes
before the leading.

An incredible thing happened when Habakkuk positioned
himself to listen to God's words: He told Habakkuk to pick up
his pen because it was His turn to talk, and His words were
worth writing down. When I think of this in my own terms, it
sounds like God would have said, "Girl, it's time to get your
prayer journal out and start writing."

Journaling is a beautiful, precious way of recording our
prayer requests and needs with God. While there are many
methods for this, I sometimes write down my words to God in
prayer. Looking back through my journal, I'm amazed to recall
what God has done. Seeing the history of your communication
with God on paper is inspiring.

God's words to Habakkuk needed to be recorded because
they would come to pass at an "appointed time." God was
saying, "Wait for me. This is not the end of the story. My timing is perfect, and it will be all you need." Then the Lord
explained to Habakkuk that his patience with the nations
wouldn't last forever, and the enemies' gods would not prevail
in the long run. He reminded Habakkuk that He still reigned

over both Heaven and Earth. "The Lord is in his holy temple; let all the earth be silent before him" (Habakkuk 2:20).

When we learn to lean into God's authority in our prayer lives, we receive the beautiful gift of hearing Him speak to our hearts. I've never heard God speak audibly, but His Spirit communes with mine and often tells me which way to go. Sometimes I've had thoughts that I knew could only be from God because I could not have come up with them on my own. The Spirit has spoken to pieces of my heart and healed them; without His promptings, the gaping wounds wouldn't have closed and scabbed over.

When I'm in the pit of despair, or like Habakkuk, wondering if it's even worth the effort it takes to pray since God isn't changing the circumstances, I remember the objective of prayer is not to get my way. Prayer aims to commune with God; when I do that, epiph-

> *Prayer aims to commune with God; when I do that, epiphanies occur.*

anies occur. I understand His Word, ways, and will on a deeper level. My trust in His sovereignty expands, and I recognize that His timing is always perfect.

Hopeful Restoration

When Matt lost his job in 2021, we cut our budget down as far as possible. We turned off all automatic bill payments because we had yet to determine where the money would come from once we used up his severance pay. Unemployment wages helped us limp through the slump, but we had no choice but to put our home on a forbearance plan to provide a little cushion while Matt looked for a new job. However, several months passed before he landed a temporary position.

The beautiful home I was sure God had given us seemed as if it would be ours no longer. I thought about the prayer of blessing our dear friends and pastors had prayed while it was still under construction. My prayer during that period of expecting to lose our home sounded much like Habakkuk's: "How long, Lord, must I call for help?"

But the many years of prayer and close communication with our Heavenly Father served as the experience I needed in that season. Most mornings, I prayed on my knees, holding my palms up to God in complete surrender. I reminded Him that everything I have in this world is His. I prayed, "Let nothing from the enemy walk through our doors. Bind him and seal the doors and windows of this house with your mercy and grace."

Two months before the forbearance plan ended, we received an email from the mortgage company about a state program that could potentially help us. Home grants were being issued to those experiencing COVID-induced hardship to help them remain in their homes, and we were encouraged to apply for assistance. As it turned out, Matt's termination date fell just within the program parameters.

We applied but were initially denied because of a technicality in the paperwork. Maybe God was having us give up our home—but I didn't feel like I was supposed to give up praying for a miracle.

So I kept praying. I asked my small group to pray. I asked my friends to pray. We needed a miracle. We knew God would have to orchestrate the details, as the situation was entirely out of our control. We appealed the denial and submitted the appropriate documentation. And we waited.

My prayer then became like Habakkuk's prayer in 3:2:

"Lord, I have heard of your fame; I stand in awe of your deeds, Lord. Repeat them in our day, in our time make them known: in wrath remember mercy."

I had seen miracles from God—everything from the tax refund that helped us buy that house to $5,000 being dropped in our backyard. I'd watched God sustain our family through that season of drought time and time again—but I needed a repeat performance. I wanted my kids to know that God cares for the birds, and He also cares for them.

I thought we would be telling our children we would have to move—but after four months, seemingly at the eleventh hour, mercy knocked at the door. An email saying we'd been approved for the program landed in my inbox, and the grant to assist our family in remaining in our blessing house was OURS! Though the wait had been long, God's timing was perfect. Once again, our prayers had been answered. I could do nothing but give Him the highest praise. God revived our home and our hope in orchestrating the details.

No Grapes on the Vine

When I read the prayers of the men and women in the Bible who longed to see God's hand move, I can feel their pain oozing from the pages. The dark spaces in life make it seem like there is no reason to pray. Sometimes the needs are so great that prayer itself feels useless—but hopefully, by now we have learned it is not.

The third chapter of Habakkuk is another prayer—but an entirely different type than that recorded in the first chapter. In the first verse, Habakkuk explains this prayer is a *shigionoth*. This Hebrew word is a literary or musical term defined as a "wild passionate song with rapid changes of rhythm."[1] Habakkuk's prayer had shifted to praise of epic proportions. Like me, he asked God to repeat the miracles he had already experienced and knew about from history, then listed them. Reading it makes me want to jump with my own joy—until I realize that even as he wrote those words, Habakkuk's situation had not changed. Enemies were still invading his nation, and God had not yet turned the tide of the war in Israel's favor.

Habakkuk still likely felt fearful to the core. His heart may have pounded; his lips may have quivered. His legs may have turned into Jell-O. He may have felt unable to breathe and devoid of all strength. But even in this awful set of circumstances, he uses the word "yet" to stop the fear in its tracks and remind his body Who is in control. It's time for a revival.

He declares,

> Yet I will wait patiently for the day of calamity to come
> on the nation invading us. Though the fig tree does not

bud and there are no grapes on the vines, though the olive crop fails and the fields produce no food, though there are no sheep in the pen and no cattle in the stalls, yet I will rejoice in the Lord, I will be joyful in God my Savior. The Sovereign Lord is my strength; he makes my feet like the feet of a deer, he enables me to tread on the heights. (Habakkuk 3:16–19)

Did you catch that second "yet"? "Yet I will rejoice in the Lord." Through prayer, Habakkuk no longer needed to experience a change in circumstances to experience change in his spirit. He chose to allow the magnitude and wonder of his God to soak into his soul. He decided to believe that the God he wanted to hear from had something to say to him. He knew that God would give him strength for whatever he faced, and whether he was walking on the peaks or in the valleys, God would hold him fast.

Prayer can move our hearts from dark spaces to hopeful places. Embrace it through difficult challenges, and you'll experience a change in heart that lasts through eternity.

God, Revive Me

God, help me enter the tower of prayer and put on my listening ears. I want to hear Your voice and know You will hold me fast. When circumstances loom large, provide my "yet."

Prompt me to remember that You are my strength, enabling me to walk both on the peaks and in the valleys.

Chapter Fourteen Prayer Principles

- Prayer isn't only about the changes we can see with our eyes and hold in our hands. Prayer is about communion with our Creator and the transformation of hearts.
- Hearing God speak to our hearts requires a willingness to step into the prayer tower and put on our listening ears.
- When we learn to lean into God's authority in our prayer lives, we receive the beautiful gift of hearing Him speak to our hearts.
- Prayer can move our hearts from dark spaces to hopeful places.

CHAPTER FIFTEEN

Beyond Survival Mode

God, Inspire Me.

I stood over her grave, fear washing over my heart again. Grieving mommas fear many things. One is that their child will be forgotten. Another is that all the valleys they've walked will become wasted wilderness. When the pain permeated my heart, I pondered, *Is this all there is to life on this planet? To suffer and die for nothing?* But I heard the Holy Spirit whisper, "This is not the end."

When a woman's husband dies, society calls her a widow. When a child survives his parents, he is called an orphan. But there is no word to describe a parent who has lost a child. This is an oversight for the ages. But as I've pondered this, a word did come to my mind: survivor. I'm guessing you might understand it as I do because you, too, are a survivor.

Whether you have survived illness, loss, grief, accident, divorce, disease, or who knows what else, you *have* survived—and despite your circumstances, you continue to live. God has breathed in your lungs, and you are still producing carbon dioxide. What does one do with the honor of living while other souls have journeyed on?

Nehemiah was a survivor who wondered the same thing. He served as a cupbearer to the king of a foreign country while worrying about his hometown Jerusalem and what might have become of his friends and family members who had survived the Israelites' exile to Babylon. When one of his brothers visited, he implored him to share all the latest news from home—but it was not good. The survivors were scraping out a meager existence. The city wall was broken down, and all the gates burnt. When Nehemiah heard the gory details, he sat down and wept.

You can guess how he felt. Beyond sad and disheartened—he was grieved. We don't know how long, but he wept, fasted, and prayed before God for some time. Nehemiah 1:5–11 documents his prayers, beginning with praise and continuing with an appeal and a confession. He quotes God's promise to reward his forefathers for their faithfulness by gathering the exiles to their homeland. He appeals to God to hear both his voice and those of others who are praying. And he asks for something unique: "Give your servant success today by granting him favor in the presence of this man."

"This man" was the king of Babylon, for whom he was the cupbearer—a position of trust and high rank in the court.

Four months passed before Nehemiah could share his heart with the king.[1] I wish the Bible told us what he did during those four months. Was he waiting for the right moment to say something? Was he so overwhelmed with grief that he couldn't think of what to say? Was he mulling over all the ideas and pondering which were his and which were God's? We don't know the answers to those questions, but we do know that Nehemiah had never been sad in the king's presence before—at least partly because that was illegal—so the king knew something was up and asked him about it. Nehemiah 2:2 explains, "I was very much afraid. . . ."

Desperation sparks fear like nothing else can. But Nehemiah admitted his sorrow to the king despite his fear. It was a big deal for him to confess this problem to his superior. The king had the power to say, "Too bad, so sad. Give me my drink," and move on to his next line of business—or have Nehemiah executed. No pressure.

Part of Nehemiah's job was to be a listener, not a broadcaster. Being vulnerable enough to share his enormous problem with the king challenged him to be courageous. But though he had good reason to fear the worst, he embraced the moment and explained his heartache.

I have to pause here to remind you that people can't pray for a problem they don't know about. They can't help you if they don't know you need help. I've also discovered that it's hard for people to help you when they don't have specifics— which can be difficult for everyone in problematic seasons when you may not be sure what you need. That's why you need time with the Lord in prayer. Face down, gut-wrenching, honest confession before God roots your relationship with Him like nothing else can.

Remember that before the king asked him why he was so down, Nehemiah had "for some days, mourned and fasted and prayed before the God of heaven." This was not a one-and-done scenario. In his written prayer, he tells us it had been a day-and-night discussion with God about the things weighing heavily on his heart and mind. He ends this prayer-filled season with a request for success and favor. That sounds like many of my dark moments praying; does it sound like yours, too?

A Little Light in the Darkness

After months of waiting, finally, the letter arrived. With my breath half-held, I ripped open the envelope, unfolded the paper, and began to speedread the words, rushing to reach the point of the letter.

Denied. The insurance company had denied our request for a special bathtub insert for my sweet Taylor. Showering her had become a herculean task of trying to wash her well while holding her up at the same time. Though she could no longer sit up alone on the shower chair, someone felt she didn't meet the proper criteria for the equipment that would have made this daily task doable.

Time seemed to stand still as discouragement poured over my heart. Why must life with a special-needs child or adult be so complicated? Why couldn't those demonstrable needs be met without the extra steps of more paperwork, more distress, more waiting?

When issues like this arose over the years of caring for Taylor, emotions would overtake me, and I couldn't think straight. But this particular letter didn't have that effect. I was finally learning how to give things to God and not let discouragement shut me down. "Lord, inspire me. Give me fresh wisdom and creative ideas to move this forward. You know Taylor needs this. You know my back needs this. Show me what to do." I immediately filed an appeal, asking God to give me the words and documentation to resolve the issue. I asked for favor and success with the insurer.

I had no idea that although we would finally receive approval for that tub insert, it would not arrive for several months. I also had no way of knowing that Taylor would take a turn for the worse shortly after it did. She never had the chance to enjoy even one warm bath inside that tub because God called her home to Heaven.

It would seem that my prayer for help had been worthless. The strategy God gave me as I wrote that appeal might seem like it was wasted. The favor I had requested could seem like it wasn't favor at all.

However, years earlier, the Lord had connected Taylor with a beautiful friend, Clara. He knew Clara would need that tub insert here on Earth once He called Taylor home to Heaven—and God gave us the privilege of giving that tub to her. My prayer for inspiration and strategy served as the answer for someone else's need. It wasn't for naught.

> *Our prayer stories are much bigger than one chapter of circumstances.*

Our prayer stories are much bigger than one chapter of circumstances.

What Do You Want?

Nehemiah, the survivor, mustered the boldness to tell the king that his hometown lay in ruins and the gates had been destroyed. In response, the king asked, "What is it that you want?"

If Nehemiah were writing this part of his book today, he might say, "Insert prayer here." Nehemiah 2:4 explains, "Then I prayed to the God of heaven. . . ." Before he responded to the king, he prayed to his God.

This is yet another Bible story that makes me I wish I were a fly on the wall in that king's court because Nehemiah doesn't tell us the words of his prayer. We only know he considered his answer to the king so pivotal that it required a conversation with God before delivering it. While this seems like a slight pause, I can't overemphasize its importance. Nehemiah's desperation for God initiated his deep dependence on God. He needed divine inspiration at that critical moment: "Lord, inspire me." He craved God-breathed wisdom and understanding.

The verb "inspire" means "to fill or produce." We're accustomed to understanding how a courageous circus act can inspire a crowd, or how an artist can move the heart of an individual. We understand this to mean being filled with emotion and awe—and perhaps moved to action as a result. But a secondary definition of "inspire" means "to inhale."[2] "Inhale" means "to breathe in, to draw in by breathing." Just as God formed the dust of the ground into Adam and then breathed life into him, so did this pause for prayer breathe new life into Nehemiah. It provided a moment to summarize what he had already worked out with God in his previous prayer time. All those days and nights of communing with God in sorrow and weeping provided the foundation for this moment. Nehemiah knew how to answer the king. He was well aware of his heart's desire. He said humbly, "I want to rebuild the city of my ancestors."

The king asked how long it would take Nehemiah to journey there and when he would return. Not only did Nehemiah answer his questions and set a time, but he made an additional request for letters to give to the governors of the provinces he would pass through on the way to Jerusalem. The king not only wrote those letters commanding the governors to provide support and supplies, but also sent his own army officers and cavalry with Nehemiah. Nehemiah must have felt like pinching himself as he rode into Jerusalem accompanied by the king's entourage.

So I'm stopping mid-story to ask: What do you want? What would you like to see happen in your desperate place of need, your hardest of hard spaces? Have you spent time with the Lord in the midst of those challenges to remember that He craves to be all you need all the time?

> *What would you like to see happen in your desperate place of need, your hardest of hard spaces?*

As I have mentioned many times throughout this book, in my most profound moments of need before God, I couldn't even think straight. My brain would not work as I wanted it to due to trauma and grief. I needed God's healing hand on my mind and His breath in my lungs. In desperation, I learned that it is only in Him that I can "live and move and have my being." The Apostle Paul tells us that God "is not served by human hands, as if he needed anything. Rather, he himself gives everyone life and breath and everything else. . ." (Acts 17:24–28).

Without the dark spaces of divorce, depression, disease, and death that I have passed through so far, I would never have been desperate enough to seek God and grow dependent on Him to breathe, live, and move. And now? I want nothing less. I know exactly what I want: I want Jesus. I want God. I want to give my whole spirit to the Holy Spirit.

Had I stood before the king in Nehemiah's place that day, would I have known what I wanted? Not without the dark, desperate spaces of learning to trust that my God is good in all things and that when I cry out to Him, I am learning to rely on Him to breathe new life into me. Without the contrasting darkness, I would not have seen the beauty of fully relying on Jesus.

Many years later, Jesus echoed the king's question to a sick man sitting by a pool in Bethesda. This disabled man had lain by the waters for thirty-eight long years, waiting for an angelic stir that supposedly held his healing. Jesus had only one question for him: "Do you want to get well?" And so I ask you the same. Do you want to experience God breathing new life into your soul? Is your prayer, "God, inspire me"?

What It Looks Like

Three days after arriving in Jerusalem, Nehemiah set out at night to examine its walls. He viewed the broken gates, blackened by fire; in many places, the rubble on the road forced him to find other avenues. Jerusalem lay in ruins. But at this point in Nehemiah's journal, nothing is written about tears, sorrow, or grief. His time of prayer and mourning before God had prepared him for determination.

Upon returning to the city's survivors and officials, he states, "You can see the trouble we're in. Come, let us rebuild, and we will no longer be in disgrace." He also told them about the favor God had given him with the king. Nehemiah boldly declared to everyone, "The God of heaven will give us success. We, his servants, will start rebuilding." Everyone was encouraged to begin this good work—and with a couple of exceptions, most did. There will always be some who doubt or even ridicule God's purpose and work in your life.

Rome wasn't built in a day, and neither were the gates of Jerusalem (though the city walls were rebuilt in a record-setting fifty-two days!). The point of this chapter is not to wish your worries away but to take them to the Lord and leave them there. But after you drop them, you can continue with praying, "God, inspire me," asking for divine thoughts that spark the best next step, even in the darkness.

The Best Next Step

Long ago, a little girl sat on the edge of her seat in a Sunday School classroom. Her teacher, Ms. Ginny, brought a pan of red Jell-O to class that morning, and the little girl could hardly wait to see what this jiggly stuff could possibly have to do with the Bible. Not to mention that Jell-O for breakfast sounded good to her.

"So the children of Israel left Egypt, and Moses led them to where God told them to go, only they were blocked in," the teacher said. "They could see the dust of the Egyptian army chasing after them, and they were frightened. But God told Moses to part the Red Sea with his staff. Moses smacked that water, and thousands walked across dry land."

That little girl was me. I imagined a young boy waving to a sea turtle in the waves as God's breath held up the giant wall of water.

Then Ms. Ginny pulled the Jell-O apart; it had been secretly wrapped in two pieces of plastic in preparation for this moment.

She had each of us walk our little fingers through the path in the middle of the "Red Sea," and I remember her saying, "God always makes a way in the wilderness."

Trek ahead forty-two years later, to the moment when I called my dad to tell him our precious Taylor girl had graduated to Heaven. He said, "You know what you need to do now?" I didn't reply but waited for his next words. "My Lord knows the way through the wilderness," he said. "All you have to do is follow."

Move ahead to the moment when the doctor asked my dad to sign paperwork instructing his doctors not to try to resuscitate him because his body had reached a point of no return to healing on this side of Heaven. Dad's response? "My Lord knows the way through the wilderness; all I have to do is follow."

When the children of Israel exited Egypt, God parted the Red Sea before their very eyes; and forty years later, when they exited the wilderness to enter the Promised Land, He did the same thing with the Jordan River. Their journey through the wilderness was bookended by these miraculous partings of water. Why did God do that?

> *"My Lord knows the way through the wilderness; all I have to do is follow."*

I think the crux of the Red Sea miracle was God showing His people that He can make a way when there is no way. But that second crossing? There was no Moses with a staff to smack the water this time; he had already passed on to Heaven. You know what parted the waters of the Jordan? The priests walked into the water carrying the Ark of the Covenant. Picture this: Joshua said, "Alright, boys. God's going to part these waters when you step in." They had to take a step of faith and believe that the God who had parted the Red Sea would part the Jordan for them. Someone had to take that first step.

Fast forward to where you are sitting right now. Perhaps you've hung onto every word I've written because desperation oozes from your soul and darkness prevails in your present wilderness. You're staring at a chilly Jordan, wondering how cold and deep the water is.

But God has not brought you this far to leave you now. While a big-picture rebuilding strategy may be more than you can think about at this moment, what might happen if you choose to take the first step into the water of trusting God? Make the cry of your heart, "God, inspire me."

God, Inspire Me

God, You are good, and I need You. Remember the promises You've made to me and redeem me again. I delight in You wholly; please bring fresh ideas into my heart and mind. Pave the way forward with favor and success because You are the divine orchestrator of all time. I trust You in this wilderness.

Chapter Fifteen Prayer Principles

- God has breathed into your lungs, and you are still living.
- Facedown, gut-wrenching, honest confession before God roots you in relationship with Him.
- Our prayer stories are much bigger than one chapter of circumstances.
- In Him, we live and move and have our being.
- Pray in desperation for God's hand to move; live depending on His heart to love.

Epilogue

"What is that?" New noises come with new homes, but this one was especially strange. The rare Saturday morning quiet elevated its oddness, and I found myself standing in the laundry room on the second floor, ear tuned to the wall. The *tik-tik* sound, which was moving, was followed by a much louder *swooshing* that I couldn't identify.

Eventually, I figured out that a living creature had entered our external laundry vent and slipped into our dryer!

When my husband arrived home, we embarked on Operation Freedom. I tilted the dryer up while he captured the animal—which turned out to be a bird—with a net and a piece of cardboard. With a houseful of teenagers, you can bet the ordeal was documented on video. Smiles and cheers followed the bird as it flew to freedom. He made it!

That's how I feel for you right now. You made it; you read this book! I hope that your deep needs have been met by hope, and your desperation has been outmatched by your dependence on God. As with the bird in our dryer, I pray that this book has launched you into newfound freedom to rely on God fully and to embrace the power of prayer in life's darkest moments.

May the following prayer replenish your soul with fresh faith and fling the gates of communication with your Heavenly Father wide open.

A Desperado's Prayer

God, see me in this desperate space.

Hold me close, Jesus; I need You.

Nothing but Your divine hand of healing will mend my brokenness.

There is no quick fix, and I need Your help.

Reassure my doubting mind.

Be my Protector, especially as I limp.

Lord, guide my every thought and prompt me to ask for directions.

You are my Refuge.

Fill my empty soul with Your love.

Show me how to see as You see.

I offer this prayer as a sweet reminder that I am Your child.

Free me that I may praise Your name.

Let me enter the tower of prayer with listening ears on; revive me.

Breathe in me as only You can,

because I trust You in this wilderness.

Amen.

Acknowledgments

Jesus, thank You for saving me, and especially for saving me from myself.

My Matthew: I can never say enough about your love and support. You are always my rock beside the Rock.

Zach, Tiff, Michael, Samuel, Tristina, Tarah, and Tessa: You are daily displays of God's graciousness to me, and I am so grateful.

Taylor, Mom, Dad, Poppy, and our baby Wojo: You are pieces of my heart and provide heavenly inspiration for earthly work. Until then.

Mary Demuth Literary & community: Thank you for your unbelievable support.

My awesome publishing team: Thank you for your hard work and commitment to this project.

To the many writing friends who have listened to the wins and woes of this project, especially my God's Girls and Ablaze groups, and Speak Up Ministries Growth Groups.

Endnotes

Chapter One: The Cry of Distress
1   "Helen Keller Quotes," GoodReads, https://www.goodreads.com /author/quotes/7275.Helen_Keller.
2   Matthew 10:30; Isaiah 49:16.
3   Henry Cloud, "How to Take Control during a Crisis," Boundaries, https://www.boundaries.me/blog/how-to-take-control-during-a -personal-crisis.

Chapter Two: Too Bitter to Swallow
1   Richard Daneman and Alexandre Prat, "The Blood-Brain Barrier," *Cold Spring Harbor Perspectives in Biology*, January 2015, 7(1), https://www.ncbi.nlm.nih.gov/pmc/articles/PMC4292164.
2   Ayana Archie and Jay Croft, "'It's Heartbreaking': Killer Whale Continues Carrying Dead Calf for 'Unprecedented' Length of Mourning," CNN, August 11, 2018, https://www.cnn.com/2018 /08/10/us/orca-whale-still-carrying-dead-baby-trnd/index.html; Mihai Andrei, "Grieving Orca Carries Dead Calf for Seven Days

in Heartbreaking Ritual," ZME Science, August 1, 2018, https://www.zmescience.com/ecology/animals-ecology/grieving-orca-calf-01082018/#:~:text=Orca%20families%20also%20have%20their,sometimes%20up%20to%20a%20day.

3   "Philippians 4:7," *Strong's Lexicon*, https://biblehub.com/strongs/philippians/4-7.htm.

Chapter Three: Pain in the Neck
1   Bruce Wilkinson, *The Prayer of Jabez: Breaking through to the Blessed Life* (Sisters, Oregon: Multnomah Press, 2000).
2   "Healing," Dictionary.com, https://www.dictionary.com/browse/healing.
3   "Jesus Healed the Sick," OpenBible.info, https://www.openbible.info/topics/jesus_healed_the_sick.

Chapter Four: Help Wanted
1   Corie Ten Boom, *Clippings from My Notebook* (Nashville, Tennessee: Thomas Nelson, 1982), 61.

Chapter Five: Chosen and Renamed
1   Biblical Studies Press, *The NET Bible First Edition Notes* (Biblical Studies Press, 2006), Genesis 17:5.
2   Rachel Wojo, *One More Step: Finding Strength When You Feel Like Giving Up* (Colorado Springs, Colorado: WaterBrook Press, 2015).

Chapter Six: Limps and Scars
1   "Some Common Phobias," Merck Manual Professional Version, https://www.merckmanuals.com/professional/multimedia/table/some-common-phobias.
2   University of Maryland, "Fear and Anxiety Share Same Bases in Brain," Neuroscience News.com, October 19, 2020, https://neurosciencenews.com/anxiety-fear-brain-17190.
3   "Jabbock River," BibleAtlas.org, https://bibleatlas.org/jabbok_river.htm.
4   Tony Evans, *The Tony Evans Bible Commentary* (Holman Bible Publishers, 2019), 86.

Chapter Seven: Directionally Challenged

1 Dictionary.com, "Destituteness," https://www.dictionary.com
   /browse/destituteness.

Chapter Eight: The Battle Is the Lord's

1 Scott Thompson, "Michael Block Sinks Hole-in-One as Dream
   PGA Championship Continues," Fox News, May 21, 2023, https:
   //www.foxnews.com/sports/michael-block-sinks-hole-in-one
   -dream-pga-championship-continues.

2 "King David Timeline," Totally History, https://totallyhistory.
   com/biblical-history/king-david.

3 Jim Maxim, *21 Days of Prayer to Overcome Strongholds* (New
   Kensington, Pennsylvania: Whitaker House, 2022), 38.

4 GoodReads, https://www.goodreads.com/quotes/148871-i-ve-read
   -the-last-page-of-the-bible-it-s-all.

Chapter Eleven: Hello, I'm over Here

1 Mary Demuth, *The Most Misunderstood Women of the Bible*
   (Washington, D.C: Salem Books, 2022), 8.

2 Roger L. Omanson and John Ellington, *A Handbook on the First
   Book of Samuel* (Swindon, England: United Bible Societies, 2001),
   35.

Chapter Thirteen: Out of the Pit

1 Matthew Henry, *Matthew Henry's Commentary on the Whole
   Bible: Complete and Unabridged in One Volume* (Peabody,
   Massachusetts: Hendrickson Publishers, 1994), 1522.

2 "Why Did Jonah Go to Tarshish Instead of Nineveh?" GotQuestions,
   https://www.gotquestions.org/Jonah-Tarshish-Nineveh.html.

Chapter Fourteen: I Need a Revival

1 Robert L. Thomas, *New American Standard Exhaustive
   Concordance, Updated Edition: Hebrew-Aramaic and Greek
   Dictionaries* (Foundation Publications, Inc. 1998), https://www
   .logos.com/product/25731/new-american-standard-exhaustive
   -concordance-updated-edition-hebrew-aramaic-and-greek-dictionaries.

Chapter Fifteen: Beyond Survival Mode
1 Stelman Smith and J. Cornwall, *The Exhaustive Dictionary of Bible Names*, (Newberry, Florida: Bridge-Logos, 1998), 257.
2 Dictionary.com, "Inspire," https://www.dictionary.com/browse/inspire.

ABOUT THE AUTHOR

RACHEL WOJO is an inspirational author, public speaker, and podcaster known for her popular blog, rachelwojo.com. Through her biblical approach and personal life experiences, Rachel empowers women to discover strength and hope in everyday situations. Despite enduring the loss of her mother, adult special needs daughter, and father, Rachel remains resilient. She has authored several books, including *One More Step: Finding Strength When You Feel Like Giving Up* and *Pure Joy: Cultivating a Happy Heart*. Rachel is crazy in love with her husband, Matt, and cherishes her motherhood with six children on Earth and two in Heaven.

Connect with Rachel
Rachel would love to hear YOUR PRAYER STORY! You can send it to her at rachel@rachelwojo.com.

Follow Rachel on Social Media
- Facebook: https://www.facebook.com/rachelwojoauthor/
- Instagram: https://www.instagram.com/rachelwojo/